A HOSEA CHRISTMAS

UNF KING THE WORLD

©

SCOTT REID

A Hosea Christmas
Unfucking the World

Copyright © 2018 by Randall Scott Reid

All rights reserved. No part of this publication may be reproduced, stored in a retrieval system or transmitted in any form by any means, electronic, mechanical, photocopy, recording or otherwise without the prior permission of the publisher, except as provided by USA copyright law.

Italics in biblical quotes indicate emphasis added.

Scripture quotations are taken from: *New American Standard Bible* Updated Edition (NASB). ©1960, 1962, 1963, 1968, 1971, 1972, 1973, 1975, 1977, 1995
by THE LOCKMAN FOUNDATION

How He Loves

Copyright © 2005 Integrity's Hosanna! Music (ASCAP) (adm. at CapitolCMGPublishing.com) All rights reserved. Used by permission.

Cover Design: Tsion Reid & Stephanie Reid
Graphic Designs: Tsion Reid, Stephanie Reid, & Scott Reid

ISBN: 9781730786365
Imprint: Independently published

Library of Congress information TBA

MY THANKS

So many wonderful people to thank, but with a title like this, I've had a caution in my spirit to name them all, lest they should face any potential backlash this book may incur...

However, there are a few, whom I am confident will take the risk! Tsion, Salem, Bethlehem Hope, and Aiden Journey Reid are the perfect people to begin with. Each of you make me the proudest dad on the planet. Every age has been my favorite. I love you.

Tsion—I mention you yet again, for your insights and suggestions into the material herein—and for your work on the cover design. You are brilliant.

Stephanie Reid, this book does not happen in a readable way without you pouring over it. To work with my life-companion and best friend to this end, is a dream I hope lasts us into heaven.

To Jen, please, please hear this: There is simply no one I would trust more than you for the final edits on this book. You get it. You hold it in the most beautiful of ways. And that means far more than I can communicate now.

To our friends who gave us a place to stay to get this written: Wow! It was beautiful and everything we needed, when we needed it.

Finally—a special thanks for our interceding friends who knew the visceral nature of this book—the potential risk involved—and encouraged us to *go for it* anyway. We love you all.

CONTENTS

FOREWORD

Ever played that party game "Never have I ever?", where you say something you've never experienced and everyone else has to switch chairs with the others who have actually done that thing? Things like: Never have I ever flown in an airplane. Never have I ever ridden a school bus to school. Never have I ever had chocolate milk in my cereal. Never have I ever broken a bone—or had a cavity—or built a snowman in November. (Great Christmas party game, by the way. You should grab your friends and throw some chairs in a circle.) Never have I ever re-gifted anything. (Careful! They will call you out if you tell untruths!) Never have I ever watched Frosty the Snowman without crying at the end when he comes back to life and yells, "***Happy Birthday!***"

Never have I ever skied this mountain I am staring at through the glass door of the lovely retreat place we've been given for the week to write (thanks to a good God and some great friends!)

Never have I ever liked onions.
Never have I ever cut my hair short.
Never have I ever watched a rugby game in person.
Never have I ever hiked a trail in high heels.

Never have I ever stopped dreaming.
Never have I ever stopped praying.
Never have I ever lost all hope.

**Never have I ever..
wanted something more than for this book that you have in your hand to be a life-change.**

Scott just asked me to write this foreword after a 24-hour editing marathon of sorts. I am pleased to and honored. I have just read through the text you have in your hand about two and a half times (once aloud to him), and I want to say:

If you are reading this in mid-to-late fall and Christmastime is really around the corner, or if you picked it up in the dead of winter, early spring, or in the middle of a scorching summer, I urge you to read it through with the eyes and heart of a child at Christmas right now. Maybe read it outloud like I just did—with the inflection you think Scott maybe was feeling when he was plunking this out with all of his heart. If you've met him, you may be able to do that easily and hear his tone of voice—if not, imagine a grown thickly-bearded man who still Laughs Out Loud at images of his brother's elated sort of primal jump-dancing in his tighty-whiteys after run-falling down the carpeted stairs at 5 a.m. on Christmas morning to discover a shiny new Go Kart!

He told this in a sermon series.
He kept the outline.
He researched some things and prayed.
He stole some time away and knocked out twelve chapters.

And it's gold. (And frankincense and myrrh!)
Christmas treasure right here.

Truth with centuries of history, an obedient prophet with a scandalous assignment (a busted and broken-up marriage to a prostitute), F**K defined and explained like you've never heard it before, the secret and SURPRISE of earth and heaven, a BUY BACK that will bring tears, and if not—I am praying for you..

A passionate telling of CHRISTMAS that tells a whole big picture story from long, long ago in a land far, far away to NOW—in your living room, around the Christmas tree or in front of the fireplace—in your favorite coffeeshop comfy chair—or trying to read yourself to sleep on your pillow tonight.

Let the story wreck you, friend, and let it UNf**k your world.

—Stephanie Reid

INTRODUCTION

Going to be honest. There is a part of me that's not looking forward to the Christmas season. Perhaps it has something to do with my current financial condition and the barrage of marketing headed my way, enticing me to desire for myself and others things I cannot afford. A two-month long irritation of capitalist theming (don't misunderstand—I happen to think capitalism a far better option than other financial systems offered by men—not perfect—just better) that invades television, seasonal movies, storefronts, billboards, weekly coupon mailings, music playlists, sports broadcasting, even well-intentioned church service projects. To be sure, there will be a few bright spots reminding us of a manger and wise men who traveled from afar—of a star on a quiet night over Bethlehem—-but they are likely to be fleeting moments between family and friend gatherings—made more difficult than normal due to holiday traffic.

Perhaps an intense twenty-nine year journey with Jesus has caused the page to turn for me. The mystery of the ultimate gift that is *Christ in me* (Col. 1:27) has come into focus, bringing the story of Adam and Eve's fall, Abraham's covenant, Isaiah and the

Prophets' vision of a coming Messiah—who came, died, rose again, returned to the Father and then re-entered earth, housing Himself in the heart of believing men—to the forefront, and has wrecked my ability to take the Western ideas of Christmas celebrating seriously. The nostalgia is no longer able to overcome the reality of what this story means to the heart of Yahweh and must therefore now mean to me.

IS THE "F" WORD REALLY NECESSARY??

An unfiltered look at the Old Testament narrative through Exodus, the Chronicles, Samuels, Kings, and the Prophets (major and minor)—say **yes.** The entire relational imagery—reality of the New Testament *bride of Christ*—demands it. Mankind is created for marital union with the Son (the Groom!) who has pursued his love. He has been faithful. We have not. We have been and continue to be a race of cheaters in the Divine relationship.

The Christmas narrative is a raw, visceral story. It is the final solution—the wooing scandal of the Divine Lover—who engages in an act so blatant in the face of humiliation, violated trust, and deserved wrath to win the heart and affection of His love, as to be forever understatedly celebrated the world over on the day we call *Christmas.*

This is no attempt at sensationalism. It's an honest endeavor to see through to the real story. Seeing it perhaps the way He sees it. We'll look at a working definition later which may help you to know this is a true intention. In the meantime, I'm hoping you'll give it a chance. If you do, I believe it will remix the Christmas story in the best of ways for you, for your family, your gatherings of worship, and your community.

IT IS A GOSPEL STORY AT ITS CORE

There is something about God-timing and man-centered earth-timing that never seem to mesh. For us, time is bound in a cacophony of moments that only seem to make a whole when we've stopped earth-living. Sometimes, our culture grants a select few a *significance* in life and accomplishments, and their moments are honored for many to see. More often than not, time (or lack thereof) can seem a threat or a burden.

Have you ever noticed that *time* never really seemed to press on Jesus? He always seemed to be so nonchalant about it. Lazarus is dying, and Jesus is in no hurry (Jn. 11:1-44). The Disciples are toiling through the night to get to the other side of the Sea of Galilea, and Jesus is content to sit and watch them struggle. (Mark 6:48)

It is a theme surrounding the Divine Person. He gives prophetic words to His prophets about a coming Messiah that none of the original readers or hearers will ever see in their physical birthday suits. Some are 600+ years in the coming. Others are 2600 years—and counting. I think it's safe to say that Yahweh does not share our time perspective. As Aslan says to Lucy in reference to His seemingly urgent needed intervention, “I call all times soon.” [1]

The more I look at the Gospel narratives, the more I am inclined to view the birth, life, death, and resurrection as one flowing, prophetic moment. From our perspective, it is a life lived over thirty-three and a half years. When we look at His life, we break it up and celebrate it as such. Hence, we have the *birth* celebration called Christmas and the *ministry, life,* and *death* part celebrated at Easter. We often forget that we are looking in on a prophetic fulfillment thousands of years in the making. Yes, the coming was a big deal, but what He accomplishes in the *whole* of the coming is what shakes the foundations of heaven in Revelation 4.

We have forgotten that the Christmas story is first and foremost the introduction to the gospel story! We typically don’t even begin to think of the gospel until Jesus is baptized by John. (Matt. 3:13-17) Yet, the *good news begins* when Yahweh breaks His 400 year silence—when the Angel comes to Zacharias and Elizabeth. (Lk. 1:11-20) It is *really good news* when Gabriel says to Mary:

“Greetings, favored one! The Lord is with you..." The angel said to her, “Do not be afraid, Mary; for you have found favor with God. And behold, you will conceive in your womb and bear a son, and you shall name Him Jesus. He will be great and will be called the Son of the Most High; and the Lord God will give Him the throne of His father

---

[1] C. S. Lewis, *Chronicles of Narnia* (New York, NY: Harper Collins, 2001), 499.

David; and He will reign over the house of Jacob forever, and His kingdom will have no end."

Luke 1:28; 30-32

And it *explodes* when the veil of the mortal world is lifted for the shepherds to see the Angelic crowd roar at the long-awaited moments that are now in motion! (Luke 2:8-15)

Were they enthralled at the preciousness of this newborn infant? Were their hearts captured at the sight of a new mother tenderly holding the fresh miracle of life in her arms?

If you read ahead to John's Revelation, you'll know this isn't the full extent of the good news. A prophetic *moment* bearing the message that all mankind had groaned for had now come!! In those early celebrations with the shepherds, we have a view behind the curtain that sees not only a manger, but a cross and a resurrection, and greater still, a mystery hidden for the ages (Col. 1:27) *revealed!*

In seeing the birth, life, death, resurrection, and pentecost as a collective singular moment in time, it will change how you celebrate. Not only how you celebrate internally, but how you process this season with your family. It will change how you live out this story with your church, and how you engage its mission with your neighbors.

The hope of the gospel—the overwhelming story of Jesus and His long-awaited coming and doings—will steal your heart as it has never done before.

I wish you a merry Christmas
I wish you a merry Christmas,
I wish you a merry Christmas
and..... [2]

---

[2] Warrell, Arthur. *A Merry Christmas*. Oxford University Press, 1935.

CHAPTER ONE

TIS THE SEASON

Despite the culture's best efforts at secularizing and *globalizing* December 25th, it remains—the world over—a distinctively Christian holiday. That doesn't mean we're celebrating it well—or really celebrating Jesus at all—yet celebrating is still happening. Thanks to the brilliance of North American marketing, we're *celebrating earlier* and *longer* than ever!

Maybe I'm alone in this, but for our American friends, have you been missing the lead up to *Thanksgiving*? I realize there are parts of our culture that have little use for the actual history of the day, but if you're over forty, you may remember that the box stores *actually had store displays*. Street lamp posts were adorned with flags displaying turkeys and Pilgrims. Town squares were replete with bales of hay under horns of plenty. Elementary schools produced *First Thanksgiving* plays. (I admit to being a little bummed that my teachers never picked me to play a Native

American. Guessing the bright blue eyes and glaring blonde hair blew the stereotype.)

These days, it would seem that Thanksgiving has been converted to the *we're "thankful" it's almost Christmas* holiday*!* Even now, the big box stores are gearing up. Halloween costumes and decorations now go out in mid-to-late August, building to a rather grotesque crescendo by October 1. However, in a relatively recent development, something rather disturbing begins to happen around mid-October, simultaneous to the Halloween decorating. With most of the outfits, make-up, wigs, plastic weapons, fake blood, fog liquid, and styrofoam tombstones picked over, and the shelving units in disarray, signs of *the season* begin to appear—BEFORE OCTOBER 31! The first trunk in the church Trunk-R-Treat has yet to yield a single piece of candy and the end caps at Walmart and Target are already overflowing with decorating trinkets. For both of these mega box stores, their garden sections are already undergoing the *Christmas* makeover. By Halloween night, the Christmas transformation will be complete.

WALMART AND DESPERATE HOUSEWIVES

I mentioned earlier my growing dissatisfaction with the overall season in the face of the slew of advertising propaganda that saturates the days of late Fall. One year in particular, the height of the *ugh* appeared mere minutes before I walked out of my door to share the story of Hosea as a *Christmas message.* It came during a children's Christmas special commercial break.

Walmart was urging me to make this Christmas *special* for my loved ones by taking advantage of their holiday deals. If they were to be believed, I could *save money AND live better.* At this *magical time of year,* who wouldn't want that—right? After all, it was Christmas time. At Christmas time, stuff is needed. They were probably right. I was going to get it somewhere. If I got it cheaper there, I could then parlay that into getting more stuff—assuming they meant from Walmart—which would in turn, up my *better-living* quotient. So glad I caught that one before bounding out of my door.

All might have been well enough had I bounded more quickly. The Walmart ad was followed by a *Desperate Housewives* trailer. Mind you, I was a mere hour from delivering a message on Hosea and Gomer's story as a Christmas story. It was a bizarre moment. **Incredulity met with confirmation.** A tendency to judge was turned to breath-stealing *knowing*. Heightening the speechlessness of those thirty seconds was the fact that it was the promotion for their *Christmas* episode.

A quick confession. The title alone, with the previous promotional spots I had seen for the show, had been enough to keep it from my TV screen. However, people talk, and by the time of the aforementioned Christmas commercial, I was well-aware of the basic premise of the production. Just to be sure it was what I thought it was—and to be fair—I have taken the trouble to read the reviews and synopsis, good and bad, of various episodes. Sadly, my earliest assumptions turned out to be accurate.

It is, indeed, a show about married couples unhappy and unfulfilled in their marital unions. Intrigue and affairs abound season after season. Christmas for these television families would be about sexy Christmas lingerie and who was cheating on whom and how *he* was dealing with it and how *she* was attempting to hide it. As I pulled out of my driveway trying to reconcile my feelings, the Holy Spirit began to counsel my emotion and thought. The words I received on the way to our rented meeting space that evening were sobering. While I could sense Yahweh was certainly not happy with the content, He wasn't apocalyptic either.

What the Father essentially communicated on that fifteen minute drive was: *Scott, the show is rather appropriate for the culture. Your world—culture—is fornicated/adulterated from Me. It's why I asked Hosea to marry Gomer. It's why My Son came.* ***The condition of your fornicated world is the backdrop of Christmas****—not Norman Rockwell's wind-driven snow of America's Victorian downtown decked in holly and lights—not presents under the tree and the delights of secretly getting them there.*

A WORLD OF NEED

For many, December 1st has become the most anticipated day in television outside of the Super Bowl. Why? ABC Family's *25 days of Christmas*! Twenty-five straight days of one Christmas special stacked upon another. Every sitcom, every made-for-TV movie, every big screen movie, every cartoon, every claymation having to do with Christmas, Santa, and New Year's Eve—running through Christmas day!

You won't have to try hard to catch the collective message. It's essentially this: There is a plot against Santa or something is wrong with Santa. He's sick, depressed, too tired, etc. Whatever the case may be, the arc of the storyline remains. Unless Santa makes the trip—brings the stuff—Christmas simply doesn't happen. The wealthy and the poor suffer alike. In recent years, the storyline has encountered a subtle shift. In the fifties, sixties, seventies, and eighties, Christmas was dependent on Santa *showing*. Beginning in the nineties, the linchpin of Christmas shifted from *Old St. Nick* to the gifts themselves.

Granted, it is still generally acknowledged that no one does gift delivery as well as he, but if something happens to the jolly fat man, then somebody has to—and can—step up to *save Christmas.* Ergo, saving Christmas = saving the toys // Santa.

I wonder to myself if this is why *How the Grinch Stole Christmas* has remained a *Christmas special* set apart all these years. **Dr. Suess challenged the meme**. The foul Grinch had given his best to keep Christmas from coming. He had even taken the last can of *who-hash* and left not even a crumb too small for a mouse. [3] The Grinch had taken it all. And so it was, on that victorious December 25th morning, the

---

[3] *How The Grinch Stole Christmas.* Directed by Chuck Jones, MGM Animation/Visual Arts,1966.

Grinch—gloating over his deed—stood aloft his hermitage home musing upon their grief when *Welcome Christmas* came floating up the sides of Mount Crumpit. The spell was broken. The glass Christmas ball was shattered. It wasn't what he nor the *Whos*—if the truth were known—would have expected, until the counterfeits had been taken. The Grinch was utterly undone.

How could it be so?
It came without ribbons.
It came without tags.
It came without packages, boxes or bags.[4]

Their wants—even their needs—had been taken, and still *Christmas came*. I would like to venture a thought. When we peel away the veneer of what the Christmas season has become, we will find *need* at its core. Even where *first-world wants* dominate, real *need* rests underneath. Yet, we must also say that it is not about need. Jesus has come and will come again regardless of our perceived needs and wants. If this seems somewhat contradictory, please pause to reconcile how it is not.

The groaning pained cry of need reverberates from Adam and Eve's fall to the present day...just not in the way or on the level that we expect or are patient enough to pay attention to. We give and we receive to alleviate need. We seek—and hope to find…to soothe—need and want. We live *in need*—yet life-living was never meant to be *about our need,*

---

[4] *How The Grinch Stole Christmas.* Directed by Chuck Jones, MGM Animation/Visual Arts. 1966.

because He has promised over and over again to meet it. The story of Jesus declares over the tired and weary world—exhausted in its pursuit of met need—to "Come to Me, all who are weary and heavy-laden, and I will give you rest. Take My yoke upon you and learn from Me, for I am gentle and humble in heart, and you will find rest for your souls. For My yoke is easy and My burden is light." (Matt. 11:28-30)

DON'T MISS THIS NEXT STATEMENT

The existence of need demands the exercise of faith. Period. Finite beings inherently require provision of some kind—some more than others. Carbon-based life forms are demonstrably the most needy. Physically, they need oxygen, acceptable food sources, sunlight, water, sleep, exercise, etc. Human types need far more. We need companionship, affirmation, love, friendship, acceptance, sex, community, homes, discipline, more....

Because these are real existent needs and not mere wants, we must also recognize what happens when these are neglected—or perceived to be neglected. Unmet need generates stress, hurt, perceived rejection, panic, and fear.

Again: *The existence of need demands the exercise of faith.*

Very few of us will idly sit by and accept the arrival of stress, hurt, rejection, panic, and fear. We *fear* the coming of any of these emotions and will do almost anything to preemptively avoid them. When we recognize that these felt and real needs are in danger of not being met, our fight or flight instincts kick in and we begin to make things happen or accept anything that at least appears to meet the need. Hence, mankind has ever been vulnerable to dangerous counterfeits and false gods offering immediate relief.

If you're not a Jesus follower and you're reading this book...if you've found yourself repulsed at the idea and very concept of *sin* and feel judged—the idea that sin makes one dirty, ugly of soul and worth—please pay close attention here...PLEASE!

Receive this biblical definition of sin—and never see or feel it the same again: *Sin is anything that hurts you or someone else emotionally, physically, mentally, or spiritually in any way, shape, or form.* That's it! Every single Levitical law and each of the Ten Commandments, when examined closely, will reveal a Father's heart that is either protecting or providing for you. To live contrary to any of these is inevitably to do real damage to you or someone else. Sin is hurt—hurt is sin. A good Father would have you and your loved ones free of it. Sin has less to do with shame and far more with serving as the diagnosis for the physical, emotional, and spiritual hurt present in your life.

And...you have probably heard that pride is the root of all sin. It may be so. However, I would like to posit a more foundational, deeper root: *fear.* Fear that real need will not be met. Impatience to have need met. The fruit of this fear? The desperate things mankind does to meet its need and the perversions that enter in as a result.

That gift-giving and receiving would become the centerpiece upon which our celebration of the birth of Jesus would rest is no mere serendipity. We give because we inherently know need and *want* exist. But what are we giving?

WHAT ARE WE GIVING?

We are giving the *relief of need*—the *satisfaction of want.* Yes, the objects themselves i.e: socks, jackets, house decorative trinkets, giftcards, and even physical paper dollars—are given, but what is actually received at the heart-level—where it matters most to the recipient—is **relief of need** and **satisfaction of want.**

If this is the case—and I'm fairly convinced that it is—I want to plant a thought in your mind that may be disturbing. Having established that *need* is real, and already knowing that *want* is a given, what happens when and if the perception of need and want become twisted and perverted beyond or even short of their actual realities? What if the perception of need and want have been unquestionably and foundationally altered as to either be desired in harmful excess and dangerous mixtures, or even in harmful *scarcity* with the same???

What happens when wants *become needs?* What happens when a want or need is placated with poisoned-laced substitutes? i.e. You wanted a quiet, relaxed mind and perhaps a sweet taste in your mouth. Rather than exercising faith, making your request known to God who would then grant you peace beyond your understanding (Phil. 4:6-7)—and maybe an apple or tangerine, you settled for a known carcinogen and now can't think straight without it. In the meantime, a tobacco company is profiting from your addiction. Obviously, it can get far worse. Alcohol and opioids certainly come to mind.

Extreme cases to be sure. So what about the mainstream? Well...have you considered the effects of what can happen when wants and needs become linked to our identities? Are you aware that Americans are statistically labeled by where they shop? I remembered being disturbed as I sat in a church plant training session and was asked to consider the demographics of our "plant target audience." *Did they shop at Target or Walmart?* was the question. The upper middle class would be found at Target—the lower middle class at Walmart. Your church budget would be impacted by where your church physically landed. If they shopped at Big Lots, you were encouraged to think well before jumping in.

A spiritually embarrassing question to answer might be: *Have you ever been embarrassed or perhaps insulted by "where" your gift was purchased?* Have you ever accused a relative or friend of being *cheap* when you discovered your gift was a *knock-off brand* or came from K-mart rather than a high-end mall store? Do you find some measure of self-respect—

even pride—in the quality of gifts you provide? If the answer is yes, it's quite possible that your identity has become merged with need and want.

You are *worth* the brand names. The *unfortunate ones* who can't afford them, may not be. The Big Lots and Thrift Store shoppers may have accepted the labels of poverty every bit as much as the rich have accepted theirs. The poor lionize their thrift and are proud to be characterized by it. The rich celebrate their extravagance and create all manner of justifications for it. But are either spiritually and physically healthy? No—probably not.

Want and desire go unchecked in both. A dear friend once sarcastically quipped to students at a youth camp that he had discovered the identity of the *AntiChrist!* He facetiously pinned the moniker to McDonald's. Why McDonald's? The Happy Meal.
Every child wants to go to McDonald's. Why? Because of the Happy Meal. What's so great about the Happy Meal? The toy. The purpose of the Toy? To make them happy! So? Ahhh! But as my friend noted, what you, the consumer, had failed to deduce was the *Happy Meal* toy has been designed by the *clown menace* himself to either break or be lost somewhere within the secret crevices of your car seats within 6.66 seconds of entry into your vehicle. Tragedy ensues for which the only cure is to go back to McDonald's, to purchase the Happy Meal, so that your child may receive the toy which will make them happy until...you get the idea. The upshot, according to my friend, was the creation of world dependency! Proof? Kid meals replete with breakable, easily lost toys are the norm for today's fast food world.

An apocalyptic theory to take seriously, it is not. Personally, this idea of serving breakfast all day long serves as a far greater threat to the world's health than the toy ever did. A threat to which my personal budget and preferences often succumb.

Humorous conspiracy theories aside, the point is frightfully valid. Need and happiness seem inextricably linked. But should they be? I've written about this extensively in *Going In Circles and Actually Getting Somewhere* and *Still Going In Circles and Getting Somewhere,* yet it bears repeating here.

Listen to Blaise Pascal's thought:

> All men seek happiness. This is without exception. Whatever different means they employ, they all tend to this end. The cause of some going to war, and of others avoiding it, is the same desire in both, attended with different views. The will never takes the least step but to this object. This is the motive of every action of every man, even of those who hang themselves.[5]

We want to be happy. To be happy, our need must be met. Our need for security, our needs for love and affirmation, our physical needs must all be met. If not, we begin to question the afore-mentioned needs. Somehow proof of our metaphysical needs being met rests upon the security of our physical needs. For many in well-economically-developed countries, that

---

[5] Blaise Pascal. *Pascal's Pensees*, trans. W.F. Trotter, (New York: E.P. Dutton, 1958), 113, thought #425.

proof rests in the security of receiving our non-vital wants.

Regardless, it is a cycle in life-living that none of us can claim to operate as fully objective observers. We are finite creatures of need. Among those needs is the emotional need of satisfaction that often translates into happiness. We want it! When we give and when we receive, we are in pursuit of these things.

WHERE HAVE THE NAME TAGS GONE?

My mom is an avid Christmas shopper for her six grandchildren, four of whom are my children. For her, it's not so much about quality, but quantity. This is not to suggest that she is giving her grandkids cheap here today-in the trash-tomorrow junk—not at all. She is a master discount, close-out, ebay, amazon, clearance scavenger! Movies, lego sets, art sets, electronic gadgets, girly hair things, action figures, video games. These kids are extravagantly loved and blessed on Christmas morning.

However, a common dilemma often occurs. With so many gifts under the tree, name tags go missing. With some of the gifts having been purchased and even wrapped two months prior, my absolutely amazing—yet occasionally absent-minded mother—has no way of accurately remembering what goes to whom. Chances are, if you find yourself opening the very same DVD you opened only moments before, it probably belonged to someone else.

That's a problem we can laugh at and enjoy. However, when we gather with the larger extended family on my mom's side, the issue takes on a more precarious relational bent that bears attending. With four sets of aunts and uncles having purchased gifts for fifteen different kids, missing name tags become an issue. Not so much in terms of who the gift belongs to, but more so, who gets credit for the gift given. If you're from a larger family, you can probably relate. Children under seven are notorious for caring little about where it came from—so long as it came. Before you have the chance to see who gave the gift, your child has ferociously torn away the ribbon and paper, tossing it upon the littered floor. Somewhere in that jumbled paper pile is the name tag that revealed the giver.

As a parent, perhaps you've endured the tense moments, wanting to teach your kids respect and gratitude for what was given. You look at your son or daughter holding their freshly opened gift, asking them with eyes wide open, "*who gave that to you?*" followed quickly by *"did you say thank you?"* Inevitably, they give you the blank stare that fully admits, "*No, I don't know who gave it to me.*" Before you can stop them, they have a tendency of blurting out, "*Hey, whoever gave this to me—thanks!*"

I think my typical response has been a red-faced apology and affirmation to the gift-giver, who almost always reveals themselves at this point, "*I'm so sorry—no doubt, they're going to love it...thank you sooo much!*"

Why does it matter? Gift-giving is often a vulnerable thing for the giver. My aunts and uncles are beautiful people. They have a genuine interest in their niece's and nephew's children. Gift-giving, when so many kids are involved, is a sacrifice. People do not like to see their sacrifices go unappreciated. While they might never admit such a thing openly, the emotional truth of it is valid. Embedded within most of us is the desire to see our gift acknowledged. Not necessarily for pride's sake—but because a desire to know if we've actually pleased the recipient is truly a fulfilling thing. Giving blesses the giver. Always has—always will. Ultimately, failure to show gratitude deteriorates relationships. The giver is robbed of needed affirmation that they gave well, and the recipient fails to receive the full impact of the love that was intimately and personally displayed toward them.

RECOGNIZING THE GIVER MATTERS

Do you remember our statement? **The existence of need demands the exercise of faith.** The great question of life and relation to the *present other* all mankind feels, is *Who's doing the giving???* What is *source* and where does *source* emanate? It's a far greater question than you may inherently think.

Source is something we tend to be beholden to. Jesus knew this to be a foundational characteristic of His creation. "For where your treasure is, there your heart will be also." (Matt. 6:21) In your pursuit of happiness and the things you believe will meet the need, a god will appear for the atheist—agnostic—pagan practitioner—Muslim and Christian alike.

Period. The atheist will make the denial, but their dependence on their chosen and attributed *source* will ultimately unmask their God-breathed soul.

Again, why does it matter? Peter warned Jesus' followers, "Be of sober spirit, be on the alert. Your adversary, the devil, prowls around like a roaring lion, seeking someone to devour." (1 Peter 5:8) A lion is a hunter. It does not hunt to treasure, but to *devour*. Yet, there is another characteristic of this hunter people of need must be made aware of. Paul writes of this hunter saying, "No wonder, for even Satan disguises himself as an angel of light. Therefore it is not surprising if his servants also disguise themselves as servants of righteousness, whose end will be according to their deeds." (2 Cor. 11:14-15)

Satan and his forces are a beguiling enemy. Consider the following for a moment:

The hunter baits the trap—the farmer fattens the turkey. Have you ever spoken kindly to your pet before caging it??? Yes—Satan is a giver of gifts. Yes—Satan gladly takes credit for good gifts if they serve to entrap his prey. Stalin was famed to instruct young Soviet children to ask God for a piece of candy. When no candy was immediately found in their hands, he replied, "Now ask me—your government—to give you a piece of candy." Entire generations of Russian, Ukranian, Romanian, Georgian, Polish, East German, Czechs, Chinese, Vietnamese, *in the absence of the correct name tag*, have been indoctrinated to give credit for life's basic necessities to those who have cruelly and scarcely handed them out. In these countries, their government leaders, through overwhelming propaganda, have become the objects of worship. As long as the lie holds, the people remain impoverished and enslaved to the state. Worse still, millions remain ignorant to the One—Jesus—who can set them free.

Are global Westerners, in particular Americans, free of such deceit? Hardly. The Satanic light shines most hypnotically there. Happiness and commercialism are blended beyond distinction. Source is not credited to Yahweh in our factual living. It is credited to dollars and the perceived sources they come from: jobs, bonuses, lotteries, gifts, inheritances, charities.

In our world, brand names and generics flourish alike and they are worshiped and held tightly for security—both physical and emotional. These brand names exist in the physical and metaphysical world. The demon god *mammon* sits above them all, supported by religiosity of the lost *church* and pagan counterparts alike.

If we're going to truly celebrate Christmas, this reality—this backdrop—is the place to start. It may sound bleak in chapter one, yet I promise that the celebration will be rather glorious by chapter twelve.

So—

God rest ye merry gentlemen
Let nothing you dismay
Remember Christ our Savior
Was born on Christmas Day
To save us all from Satan's pow'r
When we were gone astray

Oh tidings of comfort and joy
Comfort and joy
Oh tidings of comfort and joy[6]

---

[6] *God Rest Ye Merry Gentleman.* **ca. 1760** - w.m. English Traditional.

CHAPTER TWO

CHRISTMAS IN CONTEXT

Just in case you're unaware, the events that make up *Christmas* are a really long time in the making. A strong argument can be made for segueing Adam and Eve's betrayal—to Pentecost—into the Christmas story. We'll spare you a thousand years or so and focus on those days when the story begins to reach its climax. If you can believe it, that begins to happen a good 700 years before Jesus' physical birthday.

The Prophets, major and minor, scream and then whisper the event for a combined 820 years. While Jonah, Amos, and Joel certainly foreshadow a coming Messiah: Hosea, Micah, and Isaiah throw the *wow* and *wonder* of His coming into overdrive. No doubt, for those who have at least some cursory knowledge of Hosea, you're likely to be questioning that statement. I get it—Micah and Isaiah, yes—uh, Hosea?

Yes—Hosea. Hosea is a contemporary of both Micah and Isaiah. Each of these men prophesied over Israel in a window spanning from 785 BC to 681 BC. It is Micah who says, “But as for you, Bethlehem Ephrathah, Too little to be among the clans of Judah, From you One will go forth for Me to be ruler in Israel. His goings forth are from long ago, From the days of eternity.” (Micah 5:2) Isaiah echoes across time declaring, “For a child will be born to us, a son will be given to us; And the government will rest on His shoulders; And His name will be called Wonderful Counselor, Mighty God, Eternal Father, Prince of Peace.” (Isaiah 9:6)

What does Hosea say? Well, it is kind of meant to be a surprise of sorts. An unlooked for, yet declared gift. Very Christmas-esque don’t you think? To catch it, you’ll likely need an overview of what they were saying in those days. For that to make sense, you’ll need to understand the times.

MARRIAGE VOW WRITTEN IN STONE

Underpinning all of this is the long-standing covenant Israel was supposed to be honoring. Yahweh would be their exclusive God, and they would be His people. It was intimate. It was a marriage vow of sorts written in stone. Blessings and curses came in the pacted relationship. Nothing in the Prophets from Moses to Isaiah, Hosea to Micah, had been given to alter it. Yahweh, through the hand of Moses, had declared:

“See, I am setting before you today a blessing and a curse: the blessing, if you listen to the commandments of the Lord your God, which I am commanding you today; and the curse, if you do not listen to the commandments of the Lord your God, but turn aside from the way which I am commanding you today, by following other gods which you have not known." Deut. 11:26-28

There was no ambiguity to the established relationship on Yahweh's part—None. If you can believe it, *The Song of Songs,* or as most know it, *The Song of Solomon* provides the emotional bond the Father had in mind when the Abrahamic and Mosaic covenants were struck. Honor, faithfulness, fealty, loyalty, unrestrained love—were to be the hallmarks of the relationship.

The *Song of Songs* is about the lovers' attraction and pursuit of their beloved. This pursuit is the binding thread that weaves from Genesis to Revelation. He will have His treasured love, and her joy will be fully met in Him. When Hosea appears on the scene, this pursuit has become passionate—desperate—even violent. The hurt is pandemic and the need is a sea of confused want. Pure hearts are spurned—defiled hearts wallow in gladly accepted afflictions.

THE STATE OF THE NATION (OR TWAS THE NIGHT BEFORE HOSEA CAME??)

Bound by oath to the Mosaic Covenant, Israel had cheated hard. For the nation, the infidelities began early. Long before Saul, the days of the Judges saw their fair share of blessings and curses. However, the time of the Kings of Judah and Israel would be *dominated* by intensifying covenantal adultery. Of the twenty-three kings who would rule over Judah, only seven would honor the Lord. Outside of David and Josiah, even the other five "good" kings were known to tolerate in some form or fashion the existence of idols and high places within the borders.

A quick survey of the Prophets' messages that preceded Isaiah, Micah, and Hosea provide a bleak cultural picture. If you're not an Old Testament Kings and Prophets scholar, things can get a bit confusing. By the time we get to Solomon's son Rehoboam, the nation of Israel has split in two. There is the Northern Kingdom consisting of ten tribes and the remaining two tribes of Judah and Benjamin known as the Southern Kingdom, often referred to simply as *Judah.* The first prophet on record to speak to the issues of the day was Amos. Like Hosea and Micah, he has a message for the Northern Kingdom.

North America should take note. It's not what our evangelical circles tend to hyper-focus on. When Amos speaks, Israel is fourteen kings and around 132 years in. Jeroboam II now sits on the throne. If you're taking notes, none of his predecessors were good. Don't miss that. They were not bad at the "job." Economically and territorially, they had done quite well. There had been ups and downs to be sure, but for being situated between Assyria and Egypt, both the North and South had done well for themselves. By bad, I mean, *BAD people.* The North Kingdom had twenty kings in all. All of them were serial adulterers concerning the Mosaic Covenant they were sworn to uphold.

So what was happening under the reign of Jeroboam II that moved Yahweh to call a prophet to address it? *Injustice.* In many ways, both Jeroboam II of the North and Uzziah of the South had caught a break. Assyria had issues of its own, which had allowed Israel and Judah to expand territory and prosper. Due to economic and legal injustice, Israel had literally become a people of the *have's and have not's.* If you take the time to study the Levitical laws which are an integral part of the Mosaic covenant, you will find very specific laws set forth for the protection of the poor.

Debtors' prisons were never meant to be a thing in Israel. Slavery was never meant to become an institution, but rather a practical and temporary way to pay off debt. Land and homes were meant to be perpetually-inherited possessions. While you had the right to sell your property, none could permanently take it to settle debt. Under Jeroboam II and the kings preceding him, these laws had been increasingly ignored.

Amos seems rather harsh in his comparisons and descriptions. The rich had summer and winter homes, while their fellow poor Jewish citizens were bought and sold in slave labor markets. He actually refers to the wives of these men as the *cows of Bashan* (Amos 4:1). They were not exempt but rather co-defendants in Amos's charges against them. These women had coaxed and goaded their husbands to ignore the pain of the poor to increase the luxury of their personal estates.

If you couldn't pay your debts, maintain your home or fields in Jeroboam II's day, you were at risk of losing everything—even having your family scattered to the cruelties of slavery, which aided the rich in furnishing lavish estates. The *milk and honey* that had been meant for all was now needlessly hoarded and greedily obtained by men and woman living in pits of corrupted want and ill-perceived *need.*

But there was more. It was nothing new by the time Amos delivered his message. However, these were not the early days in the wilderness. These were not the days of the Judges when existing in the land was a life and death struggle. David and Solomon had left this people strong and relatively secure in their borders. They had *things* now. How they handled their possessions and responsibilities before Yahweh could not be hidden. Falling for deceptive gods in desperate days and brutal hours is bad enough. Receiving and crediting them in the face of blessing is nearly cataclysmic for the Divine relationship.

I must conjecture a bit next, as there is admittedly very little concrete evidence for dating Joel's writing. It only seems certain his message is meant for the Southern Kingdom. If indeed, his writing is contemporary to Amos as a counterpart to the North, Yahweh's slow kindling anger is boiling over. Not anger for an enemy. That is something altogether different. This is the hurt that comes from the betrayal of your love. Promises of faithfulness and provision in the face of grace and blessing spurned—rejected—ignored. Wrath at seeing a prized treasure broken, tarnished, soiled—by choice. Such as mankind has been wont to be, taking for granted the romantic pursuit of the Divine Lover, Joel is a message of Divine response from the cultural demise among the covenant people. Judgment is coming. He will not leave His love to suffer and die from perpetual self-inflicted wounds. *He will act.*

ENTER HOSEA

When Hosea, a citizen of the Northern Kingdom, comes on the scene a decade later, the same injustice is rampant. However, things with the powers to the North and South are not so good. While the people continue to live in wealth that is tenuous, it is now under obvious threat. Hosea's time is marked by political upheaval as a succession of rulers attempt to find their security in brokered deals with enemies who do not have their best interests at heart. In view of these times, a dark evil is once again prominent in the land. The *Baals* and *Asherah* poles have returned. The deep offense of the worship of Baal to Yahweh cannot possibly be overstated. It's why we took the time to recognize the existence of need earlier in chapter one. Remembering that sin carries real pain, pay attention to the details of Baal and Asherah.

BAAL AND ASHERAH

All of it centers around need—perceived and real. Baal is usually found as a wooden or stone image of a man with a lightning bolt in hand with horns coming from his helm—kind of like Elmer Fudd when he sings *Kill the wabbit* in *Looney Toons.*[7] Asherah is sometimes found as a large totem pole, while at other times, she is fashioned as a handheld version, usually depicted as a naked woman holding her breasts.

---

[7] *What's Opera Doc?.* Chuck Jones. Warner Bros. Cartoons, 1957.

In Canaanite mythology, these two are worshiped and credited for all things regarding fertility. This extends to finances, as well as to agriculture and physical offspring. The essential object of their worship is to entice Baal to have sex with his mother, Asherah. When they do, sons are born—good harvests can be expected—plenty (finances) will flow.

How do they entice this incestuous relationship? The answer is found in varying degrees of degradation. In its mild and initial forms, animal sacrifice—small to large—is expected. When these small measures fail, or when communities are deeply committed to the cult, sexual intercourse with priestesses of Asherah—temple prostitutes—may be required. This had a way of becoming an egregious burden, as the men were encouraged to offer up their daughters to *service* the men who worshiped at these temple sites. Additionally, as seen in Elijah's confrontation with the priests of Baal and Asherah on Mt. Carmel, cutting and self-mutilation mixed with incantations and screams were practiced (1 Kings 18). The most extreme versions of this cult were found—possibly mixed—with the Ammonite god Moloch. Jeremiah, among others, refers to these (Jeremiah 7:31, 19:5). Often portrayed as a last resort, cult practitioners were encouraged to sacrifice their firstborn children to gain the favor of Baal or Moloch. This was achieved by placing their son or daughter in the arms of the Topheth. The Topheth was a large stone image with arms extending over an open fire. The children were burned to incite *needed* blessing or intervention.

Why? Because they needed rain. Their crops and herds depended on it. They needed children—sons, in particular—to care for them in their old age. Too often, we make the mistake of visualizing these peoples engaged in parties and careless orgies. Sanguine personalities giving their bodies to pleasure without fear or remorse—one big frat bizarre. And so we miss it. We don't make the real connect in their day or ours.

It wasn't a party. It was a way of life. It was the way to survive. Like you and I today, these Jewish people were simply trying to make it—keep the bills paid, the kids fed, retirement futures secure, convenience available, leisure possible, crises at bay—at all costs. *Don't miss this.* Middle Eastern culture, even to the present day, does not recognize the mythical divide between the secular and the religious. There were demonic gods represented by Baal, Asherah, and Moloch. They gave and they took away. It was real. Service and credit had to be rendered. And so they did—ignoring the One who was truly responsible for providing for them all along.

A SEASON OF FEELING

Yahweh was about to do something in Hosea's real time that would both devastate and enrapture his world. It was a *see how it feels* season. Hosea is a real life-lived story, where Yahweh revealed His heart emotion in the most vivid way possible. We're about to walk our way through it. When we get to the end, you will hear the Christmas celebration in a visceral shout over it all.

Those expectant days (our celebration of the Christmas season—those days walked before the Christ child was laid in a manger)—should be felt in our souls as hard days when Yahweh brooded over a world that had spurned His gifts, His romance, His security, His friendship, His countless kindnesses, His very existence in lieu of counterfeits and generics that neither satisfied nor saved, but rather killed.

CHAPTER THREE

HOSEA IN A MARSHMALLOW WORLD

Hosea is about to be married and should be anticipating the sweetness of a honeymoon and happily ever after...

Yet, Hosea chapter one verse two has an ominous beginning, and it's anything but marshmallow-y. It reads, "When the Lord first spoke through Hosea, the Lord said to Hosea, 'Go, take to yourself a wife of harlotry and have children of harlotry; for the land commits flagrant harlotry, forsaking the Lord.'"

At first glance, if you understand the integrity of real Old Testament prophets, this can't be happening. It's been a problem spot for translators for centuries. While some have suggested that Hosea's marriage is pure allegory, the remainder of the story argues against it. More than a few have been willing to take the chronology at face value. Hosea is told to marry a prostitute—possibly an Asherah temple prostitute—for a wife.

However, a more prominent understanding suggests that Hosea is committing to paper his experience in hindsight. Therefore, it is probable that Gomer was, at least to Hosea's knowledge, *chaste* when they were first married. Hosea's understanding of Yahweh's omniscience considered, he's writing as if God has told him to marry Gomer, knowing full well the infidelities she will subject Hosea and herself to in the future…a kind of spoiler alert to let the reader know what Hosea will soon have to endure.

If you're wondering if it matters—apart from the allegory perspective—the answer is most likely not. Why? Because he obviously loved her. She may have *turned a trick* the week before, or found herself *a desperate housewife* a year in. Regardless, Hosea took her for a bride, and if the verses that follow are any indication, he had totally fallen for Gomer.

FALLING APART

I've performed my fair share of weddings and premarital counseling. For most, the first year is hard. For a few, it is absolutely brutal. I once had a couple call me from their honeymoon while in Disney's Epcot. The groom was breathlessly chasing his bride through the park shouting on the phone, *"Tell her to submit, Scott*! *Tell her she has to submit*!!!" Remarkably, though I could tell she was some way ahead, I could hear the bride screaming back over the groom's demands, *"When we get back, we're getting a divorce!"* All with embroidered "his" and "her" honeymoon Mickey ears atop their wedded heads. Happy ending, however…as nearly twelve years later (as of this writing), they're still together with two of the most adorable and brilliant children I've ever met!

For Hosea, things seem to fall apart rather fast. You catch it in the naming of their children. Names were important in Middle Eastern culture. John, Brian, Cindy, Alicia...are nice enough, but often times, parents in our modern day culture do not give a lot of consideration to meaning. Typically, birth names really serve no other purpose than to *have a ring to them* when combined with their full names. It's more about not embarrassing your kid in elementary and middle school. Not so in Jewish culture. Names were descriptive and prophetic in nature. The name of Hosea and Gomer's first child makes quite the statement.

JEZREEL

To my knowledge, there is no way to know how long they were married before baby number one arrives, but I'm guessing it was relatively soon. Immediately, Yahweh comes to Hosea, giving the child a significant name connected to the not-too-distant past of the Northern Kingdom. The prophet Elisha had anointed Jehu to take the throne from a man named Joram. Joram was the son of Ahab, and that is very important to this story. It was Ahab who sanctioned a full-throated support and implementation of Baal worship into the Northern Kingdom through the influence of his wife Jezebel. Jezebel was a high priestess of Asherah and evil to her core. Even though Jezebel's priests and prostitute priestesses had been humiliated and annihilated by Elijah (1

Kings 18:40). Ahab's predecessor, Joram, showed no signs of backing off. Jehu is commissioned to kill Joram, Jezebel, and everyone connected to Ahab's house (2 Kings 9:7). However, when Jehu finds Joram in the valley of Jezreel, he goes a bit overboard and kills Ahaziah, the king of Judah as well. It is this unsanctioned slaying, for which Jehu's dynasty must answer.

However, given the meaning of the name, I think we can see further in. The name literally means *God plants.* While the name of this child points to a future judgment for a ruling family, it also serves to remind a culture who had neglected, if not forgotten altogether, the One who is doing the providing. At the time of this writing, many in the land are sacrificing the gifts Yahweh had given them to Baal to receive the things only Yahweh provides. Some of them are making the required sacrifices to Yahweh on Saturday and engaging in sexual intercourse with Asherah prostitutes on Sunday, hoping Asherah would bring sons into their homes. Meanwhile, a broken-hearted *El-Chuwl (the God who gave birth) says* over his people, "*No beloved, I planted. I brought the rain. I brought the harvest. I made the sun to shine. I fashioned your bodies to procreate life. I do these things and no other.*"

Their first child is in the home, and there seems to be strife already. Later on, we'll catch Gomer participating in the Baal cult. Could it be that her sympathies are becoming known to Hosea early on? Could Hosea's message find its initial audience under his own roof? Has a doubt arisen from his bride about the essential question that matters—*"Who is doing the providing?"* By the time kiddo number two arrives, things have obviously gone relationally critical.

LO RUHAMAH

Bearing in mind that Hosea's experience is following Yahweh's heart, we can assume Lo Ruhamah's name has significance in Hosea's day-to-day living. It literally means "not loved" (Hosea 1:6). Being a father of four—three boys and a girl—there are certain foundational needs that the sexes require in greater emphases. My sons need to know that I'm proud of them. Yes, they want to know that I love them, but for them to know that I love them, I must show my pride over them. However, my daughter needs to know that I love her—no matter what: bad hair day, emotions scattered, clothing dilemmas, I love her just the same. Again, for sure, she wants me to be proud of her, but for her to have belief in my pride over her, I must demonstrate my love for her. It's simply the way it is.

Lo Ruhamah is Hosea's middle child and his only daughter. I can't think of a more devastating label for a little girl to carry through her childhood and teenage years than the name *Unloved.* If you can, you'll have to forgive Hosea, it is the name that Yahweh has given her for the time and circumstances she lives in. It more represents his relationship with Gomer at this time than with his little girl. However, because of the bitterness that is developing between the two, it's quite possible that Hosea is frustrated with everything to do with Gomer and sadly, as is all too common, it spills over to the children.

Hosea loves Gomer. He desperately wants to be the man who meets her needs. But for whatever reason, Gomer is unsatisfied. Not only is she unsatisfied with Hosea, she is unsatisfied with Jezreel and Lo Ruhamah, unsatisfied with Yahweh, ultimately, unsatisfied with life. Hosea wants to love her, *but he can't*, because he isn't loved in return, but he *does* (love her)...It's a maddening place to be. However, it's about to get far worse. The bottom is falling out.

LO AMMI

While the births of Jezreel and Lo Ruhamah seem to be close in proximity, the arrival of Lo Ammi comes a few years later. Gomer does not become pregnant with her third child until she had weaned Lo Ruhumah. In 6th century BC world, this could take up to three years or even more for some. The name is life-shattering. It means *not my people.* A more intimate version for Lo Ammi meant "not mine."

There is some debate as to what this might actually mean for Hosea and Lo Ammi. Given the fact that Gomer will shortly be found out of the home pursuing other lovers (2:5), some suggest that Lo Ammi really isn't Hosea's at all, but rather the result of an affair. The truth of the matter will have to wait for heaven. At the least, it is highly likely that Gomer had had an affair—maybe more than one—and the true biological father is simply unknown. Lo Ammi may actually belong to Hosea—he may not. Regardless, given a son's need for affirmation, how would you like to go through life with that label?

Can you imagine? *"Hey Carl, who's that young fella you have with you?"* Poor Lo Ammi, staring up into his dad's face, having to hear the rejection, *"Not mine"* = awkward—for everyone.

Again, the name seems aimed more at Gomer than his son. Every time he or anyone else would call the child's name in the presence of his mother, she would be reminded of her infidelity. It was a name that cut.

You may be relieved to learn that while their given names are recorded by Hosea, there is some evidence that he may not have used them when speaking directly to them. Verse two of chapter two reads, "Say to your brothers, 'Ammi,' and to your sisters, 'Ruhamah.'" You'll notice the "Lo—Not" are missing from their names. If this is so, then the fathering heart of Hosea takes on a whole new dimension. As far as Gomer is concerned, their names are *Not Loved* and *Not Mine.* But for Hosea, in the intimate environs of their home they were called *Loved* and *Mine*! Their mother could play the harlot, but that didn't change how he felt about them forever. He may have held rage and anger at the outset that splashed upon their arrivals, yet the love of Yahweh has a way of coming out of the people who love Him.

Hosea is still hurt. He's still a jilted, cheated-on lover and husband—but at least his hurt isn't landing on the wrong places.

CHAPTER FOUR

I SAW MOMMY KISSING WHO??

Were you aware that the Northern and Southern Kingdoms had six cities of refuge between them? (Exodus 21: 12-14, Numbers 35: 9-34, Deuteronomy 19:1-13, Joshua 20)? Did you know, further still, that part of their function was to be a place of refuge for jealous men who had killed or badly injured their wives and adulterating lovers? Crimes of passion have long been *a thing.* Yahweh, operating in mercy, foresaw the need for such cities in lieu of the cultural adultery that abounded in Hosea's day.

When we come to Hosea chapter two, he is found in a jealous rage. It opens with Hosea asking his kids to speak with their mother. He is passing on words of warning to Gomer. Perversion may have been ruling in the land, but the law of Moses still held.

Gomer is no longer living in the home. We're not exactly sure what is happening other than she appears to be latching on to anyone who will give her the things she desires. What are the *things?* Much of these appear to be household basics: bread, water, flax, oil, wine, and wool (2:5). However, verse eight makes it clear that currency is involved. Reading between the lines, we may begin to see that Gomer is finding men who will give these things in excess, in exchange for what she can give them—her body. Did that make her a professional prostitute or an opportunist? It's hard to tell. Whatever it is, Hosea is ready to utterly humiliate her.

When you read verse eight, you will begin to understand. It says, "For she does not know that it was I who gave her the grain, the new wine and the oil, and lavished on her silver and gold, which they used for Baal." Maybe you're catching it, and maybe you're not.

He loves her, he hates her, he loves her, loves her, loves her. Never satisfied, never believing, she became vulnerable to those who would use her. Indications from verse eight, in light of the context that follows it, suggest, at the least, he is the latest in a line of others. However, because she has become property (3:2)—possibly of the man silently alluded to in 2:8, she is likely now to be nothing more than a sex slave.

Imagine, if you will, Hosea often watching Gomer from afar. She had left him for the empty promises her lovers offered to her. It's obvious the lifestyle is taking its toll. Her body bears the marks of hunger and her clothes are ragged. The men in her life are getting what they want from her and she is getting little in return. Hosea, still caring for her need, does the unthinkable. Knowing she will not accept it directly from him, he approaches the man his emotion would rather have slain on the spot, but rather gives him food, material for clothing, wine, even money—to care for his wife.

Can you feel his rage when he watches from a distance as Gomer wraps her arms around the __(expletive!)__ that had nothing to do with the gifts, yet takes credit for all of them? Furthermore, can you feel his breath leave his chest when he learns that the money he has given them is spent honoring and inviting the demonic presence of Baal? There is nothing incomplete about Gomer's violation of the marriage covenant.

Hosea now knows full-on the heartache of Yahweh. From Exodus through the lives of David and Solomon, His faithfulness has been declared by wonder upon wonder—Yahweh's care and miraculous provision over Israel, and still she cheats. The Gentiles (everyone else) are not exempt. Placed on a life-sustaining planet, with the testimonies of God-fearing men evident in all generations (Adam to the present day), still man would rather worship/*depend on* various existing idols rather than HE WHO IS.

BACK TO THE NAMES

The names of Hosea's children are utterly appropriate. In the face of real need and a real devil who would take advantage of it, Yahweh has ever proclaimed and shone Himself faithful. He shouts to His creation:

"I plant! — I harvest!
You're making Me want to 'Not Love' you.
You act as if you were 'Not Mine'...

But...

I do love you...."

And then...

EXPLOSION

I'll let Hosea say it:

> "Therefore, I will take back My grain at harvest time and my new wine in its season. I will also take away My wool and My flax given to cover her nakedness. And then I will uncover her lewdness in the sight of her lovers, and no one will rescue her out of My hand. I will also put an end to all her gaiety, her feasts, her new moons, her sabbaths and all her festal assemblies. I will destroy her vines and fig trees, of which she said, 'These are my wages which my lovers have given me.' And I will make them a forest, and the beasts of the field will devour them. I will punish her for the days of the Baals when she used to offer sacrifices to them and adorn herself with her earrings and jewelry, and follow her lovers, so that she forgot Me," declares the Lord.
>
> Hosea 2:9-13

To get the full effect of the explosion, it may help to back up and read verses two through eight. It's not encouraging. Hosea is livid, and who can blame him?

THE BITTER CUP

Did you know that Israel had a law concerning jealousy? It's not so much a law as it is a procedure—a test to determine if the husband has anything to worry about. I must warn you, however, if it turns out that what the husband fears is true—that his wife has had sexual intercourse with another man—the consequences of the test are rather harsh. You can read about it in Numbers 5:11-31.

It essentially says that if a man suspected or had good reason to believe his wife had cheated on him, he could bring her to the Temple to undergo the following test: She would stand before the priest with an offering of grain in her hand. The priest would ask her to take an oath swearing to her innocence. She would then be made to drink holy water infused with dust from the Tabernacle floor from a clay cup. If she was dishonest about her adultery, this drink would carry a curse which would cause her abdomen to swell and her thigh to shrivel. Nothing is said regarding how long it would take for these symptoms to occur. I'm only guessing it would be painful and unattractive either way. It has become known simply as *the bitter cup.*

Hosea's love and care for Gomer is brilliantly demonstrated by the fact that Hosea never even suggests that Gomer undergo the legal remedy that is available to him. He refuses to do this to her. We forget that Hosea, like most prophets, would have been well-known and well-respected in the community at large. Prophets were kind of like Tolkien's wizards.

They were not to be trifled with. The public humiliation Gomer brings upon Hosea and her children cannot be overstated in this culture. In the annuls of history, had Gomer been dragged before the priest to drink the cup, it's doubtful we would have ever learned of it. *That she didn't,* is what begins to make this a *Christmas story.* It kind of makes me want to sing a Christmas carol or two...but what to sing???

A CHRISTMAS SONG

Have you ever made the mistake of starting the Christmas music way too early? You catch that fleeting glimpse of unseasonal winter cold in October, and you simply can't help yourself. Your favorite Christmas albums come out—which would be fine and dandy if you weren't sick of them by December 17th. However, there is one song that wasn't written for Christmas—that I have adopted as a Christmas song and continue to enjoy all the live-long year—but especially so at Christmas.

It was late July in the summer of 2009, when a very special song came into focus for me and the small group of students I was leading on a summer mission outreach in St. Pete Beach, Florida. It had been a full day of preparations for a three-day worship experience we were to present at Pasadena Community Church. As the sun went below the rim of the ocean, we sat in a circle on the gym floor, surrounded by stage platforms, lighting, and sound equipment. Quietly, with the soft sounds of an acoustic guitar, this song was lifted:

He is jealous for me
Love's like a hurricane, and I am a tree
Bending beneath the weight of His wind and mercy
When all of a sudden
I am unaware of these afflictions eclipsed by glory
And I realize just how beautiful you are and how great your affections are for me
And oh
How He loves us oh
Oh how He loves us
how He loves us oh[8]

John Mark McMillan

A song the church has sung for years now—until we forgot the depth and meaning of the lyric. Today, when I think of Gomer—and I often do—I think of *How He Loves.* That Yahweh is *jealous* for me. Like Hosea, His jealous rage comes after and for me like a hurricane. The wind and waves of his disciplining love press me to the ground and in those moments—sometimes seasons—the beauty of the One Who is *Other* breaks forth in His felt affections for me and I am undone and overcome. OH HOW HE LOVES!

In the face of my personal adulteries of heart that have sought to meet need apart from Him, I often hear a hard voice—not void of love, but violently shaking with it:

"You are mine.

---

[8] John Mark McMillan. *The Medicine.* Integrity Music – 48152. 2010. Compact Disc.

Don't you know whose you are???

You are mine!"

In this real-lived story, it's Yahweh shouting through the heart and emotion of Hosea to Gomer:

"I Plant!—
I don't love you (but I really really do)—
you're not mine (but you really are..........)

It's these conflicting emotions that get us to the Christmas part of the story. The part of the story that may make *How He Loves* your new favorite Christmas song.

CHAPTER 5

THEREFORE...FA LA LA LA LA LA LA LA LA

When we last left Hosea in chapter two, he was still raging fanatically his raw intentions toward Gomer. However much earned or deserved, they were not pretty or nice. But then, on a dime—he shifts. In verse thirteen, he had just said he was going to *punish Gomer* for her dedication to Baal. We all know why now. And then—verse fourteen changes everything. The entire story up to this point takes an immediate turn. Hosea was going 200 miles an hour in rage—and turns—without shifting, breaking, using a turn signal, *anything*. If it had been a car, no one would have had a head left on their shoulders.

It says, "Therefore, behold, I will allure her." (2:14) Upon first *and* second glances, I needed an explanation for the *therefore* and *behold* in the text. *Behold* makes sense. It's an attention-getter. It is a way to say to everyone who may be falling asleep in the story, "*Hey!...Stop what you're doing and pay attention to this. Look at me. You don't want to miss this.*" It is a way to announce a wow about what comes next. Absolutely, *behold* belongs in this sentence. But *therefore? Therefore* is there to connect a shift in the context or to cause precedent. *"In lieu of what has just been said, 'this' will now take place."* Therefore should make sense. What Hosea says after *behold* does not gel with the jealous rage witnessed in the previous thirteen verses.

What would make sense would be the *bitter cup* in front of the priest in the presence of Yahweh who would bring justice. Not suggesting capital punishment is ever a good idea in these matters, yet in this culture and time period, it wouldn't have been unexpected or surprising.

What does he say? *I will* ***allure*** her (v.14)? Really? Not sure what inspired me to do it, but I double-checked the usage of *allure* in this specific passage. The Hebrew *pathah,* transliterated into English, carries the following ideas: to entice, to deceive, to seduce.[9] You find its use in Exodus 22:16 in regards to a man seducing a virgin. In Judges 14:15, the word is used when Sampson's wife is asked to entice her husband into telling a secret. It is an altogether romantic—even playful—imaging word to be used by Hosea in this moment. Yet, in the face of Gomer's adultery, it is abruptly there.

What did we say? Hosea loves this woman. Good, bad, indifferent—he can't help himself. He has to do anything and everything to win her back.

---

[9] *The Strongest NASB Exhaustive Concordance,* (Grand Rapids, MI: Zondervan, 2004), 1459.

CHRISTMAS MORNING//SURPRISES & GO KARTS

If I can help you to read verses fourteen through twenty-three well, it may astonish you. We are watching an almost giddy Hosea say to Gomer, *"Gomer, beloved, I have a surprise for you. I see you where you are, and I can't wait to show you what I am about to do for you. You'll never guess it in a million years. I love you so much. I'm going to win you again. Just wait and see. I've got something for you...."* These verses are Hosea's secret plans to do just that.

ISN'T IT THE SURPRISE THAT MAKES CHRISTMAS SO MUCH FUN?

No one, to my knowledge, has done as much to make the mystery and surprise of Christmas a greater anticipatory event than my mother. Constance Ann Reid was relentless! She once had my uncle position an extension ladder from a deck to my bedroom window, which was three stories off the ground if you included the basement. With flashlight in hand, shining on a fake white-bearded face and K-mart -purchased Santa hat, he peered into my window as my mom and aunt were tucking us in for a long Christmas Eve night. The poor man nearly broke his ankle scurrying down the ladder as my aunt swiftly tackled both me and my brother to the ground, keeping us from learning their hastily and ill-planned shenanigans for keeping *Old St. Nick* alive and well in our imaginations.

As a young teenager, my mom let me in on the fun of making one particular Christmas morning a holiday celebration my younger brother Jeremy would never forget. The Christmas prior, our first cousins had received fuel-powered remote control cars. Neither of us had ever seen anything like them. Ours were battery operated. By battery, I mean eight double A batteries in the car and another four in the controller, which netted you about twenty minutes of real playing time before they had to be put back in the charger. Running on some kind of alcohol-based fuel, these things absolutely flew—so fast, in fact, that they were prone to rather intense wrecks and needs for significant repairs.

I'm not sure the time of year—it was likely early August—Mom and Dad had begun the traditional inquiries as to what we would be *asking Santa for* Christmas. Jeremy's *dream-ask* was a Go Kart. Some others in the neighborhood had received theirs over the past couple of years, so the need and desire in my little brother was deep and sincere. He knew it was a big ask, so he wasn't altogether depressed when Mom and Dad encouraged him to think of something a bit smaller. "Santa", they said, "couldn't fit things like that on the sleigh. Perhaps we should come up with something that would take less room." After briefly giving it some thought, he settled on a remote control car—"or something like that."

You may be thinking he gave up a bit easily. Not at all. While our family was certainly not poor, neither were we wealthy. We were a *middle of the middle class* family. When you grow up there or below, you understand quite instinctively that some gifts are either too good to be true or at least on the edge of being so. When you can't have them, you're really not altogether upset about it, as they're really more fantasy than anything else. That fact, is what makes this tale so fun. The Go Kart was the gift Mom and Dad had in mind for Jeremy all along. He would never see it coming.

As the early days of November came, so did the anticipation for Christmas. Our family has traditionally begun the Christmas season by putting up the tree on Thanksgiving evening while listening to Christmas records. With my mom's ok, I was granted permission to engage in a bit of subterfuge with Jeremy's Christmas expectations. What did I do?

I told him that indeed he was to receive a remote control car—but not just any remote control car. A gas-powered remote control car. It was going to be the most amazing Christmas morning he had ever lived! Jeremy Shawn Reid was lit up. As the weeks passed and the wrapped presents began to accumulate under the tree, I continued to drip salacious details about the remote controlled car of all remote control cars. Above all, it was fast. *"Dad and I tested it in a parking lot the other day and it went sixty miles an hour!... I'm serious, man! You're never going to believe how amazing this thing is...."*

Jeremy, being five years my junior, ate it up. He couldn't believe it. Of course, I had sworn him under threat of an intense beating that he couldn't let on to Mom and Dad that I had told him ANYTHING! It was a secret of utmost importance. The *happy* of the day depended on it. So serious was Jeremy about the details of this secret, that his precious ten-year-old little mind didn't so much as breathe it to his most intimate of friends. It was our private and frequent joy for those thirty days in November and December.

Can I tell you that I have no memory of what I received that Christmas? I was so excited to experience Jeremy's surprise that I couldn't sleep. It couldn't have been much past 5 a.m. when Jeremy and I met at the top of the stairs, waiting for Mom and Dad to go down before us to get the lights and cameras ready for our initial reactions. It felt like forever. Even now, I can hear in my mind the rustling and clanking from below—the smell of coffee wafting up the stairs saying good morning.

All the while, I continued to pour it on thick. *"Man, are you ready for this?...I'm telling you—sixty miles an hour!"—"Are you serious, Scottie.... I can't believe it... I can't believe it."* I distinctly remember being sure to be the first down the stairs so I could watch my brother freak. When he reached the bottom of the stairs and turned the corner to our living room, he did not disappoint. Dressed only in his Fruit of the Loom *tighty-whiteys,* he was a sight to behold.

Never have I ever seen a child more undone in his bewilderment and excitement than Jeremy in that moment. It was as if he had lost all control of his vocal chords, limbs, and facial muscles. It was the most undignified response ever loosed in the presence of another. Dancing—prancing—hopping—I honestly have no idea what you could call it. Jeremy, laughing with inaudible expressions, leapt into the seat of the orange Go Kart, jerking at the steering wheel, while somehow bouncing from his seated bottom. He simply couldn't contain himself. The son of Randy and Connie Reid was undone and beside himself at a gift he never could have imagined he would have ever received. The Go Kart had been a nice fantasy. One that you were wise to remove from mind and heart as days like Christmas drew nearer. But there it was. It was his. He was loved and he knew it. At his core, he knew it.

THE SURPRISE…???

And so, for Gomer, the *surprise* is hanging in the air. Trapped by the *lover* who never really had anything to give her in the first place, she has been reduced to mere property. You'll notice that Hosea has cut off the flow of provision that Gomer's lover had been taking credit for (2:9). Baal, as it seems, is of no use when Yahweh withholds the goods that its hidden demonic *influence peddlers* dole out for favors. Gomer has lost her mystery, charm, and attraction to the men that *need* to use them.

I try to imagine Hosea's thought when he learns that his prostituting wife is up for sale. I can't. What do you do with that? In a grace that foreruns the cross of Jesus, Hosea is told exactly what to do. It's time to reveal the mystery of the surprise. He's going to buy her back! Hosea 3:1-2 records it like this:

> Then the Lord said to me, "Go again, love a woman who is loved by her husband, yet an adulteress, even as the Lord loves the sons of Israel, though they turn to other gods and love raisin cakes." So I bought her for myself for fifteen shekels of silver and a homer and a half of barley.

Do you remember our mention of the *bitter cup* in Numbers 5? It really helps to do so. While the culture has degraded, there is still a degree of legalism when it comes to the Jewish law. Like pastors and their families today (or at least twenty years ago), who lived with certain behavioral expectations that usually centered around abstinence—from tobacco, alcohol, Rated R movies, perverse language and *swear words*—so we can understand Hosea's community position. Hosea's family, wife included, was expected to behave. If they didn't, Hosea was fully expected to engage in the remedies that the law of Moses provided. Expectation is too light a word here. Hosea is a man under a microscope. Prophets, pastors, teachers almost always are. People are looking to see what he will do—and certainly had opinions on what they thought he should do.

Risking and enduring great humiliation, he shocks everyone—including his wife. You can be sure no one in Hosea's circles or Gomer's expected this. The most surprised of all—Gomer. She was supposed to drink the *bitter cup.* In so many ways, it is Hosea who drinks the bitter cup of embarrassment and communal humiliation. Yet, it is the way he does it.

When Hosea comes to close the sale—which sounds ridiculous to even write—she is let go at a slave's bargain. Literally. Hosea pays in grain. It measured out to about fifteen pieces of silver. It was the going rate for a common slave at that time. And he makes Gomer his own. Through loving discipline and a wooing heart, he will and does finally win the heart and devotion of his beloved Gomer. *Surprise!!!*

There is no way that I can ever be convinced that Gomer saw it coming. Even in those moments when Hosea paid out the grain to purchase her, I doubt little that she was filled with dread. Fear of revenge and retaliation had to be on her mind. That he would seek to elevate her to a cherished and treasured wife was something her heart would never have expected and would never recover from. Coming back to my favorite *Christmas song:*

We are His portion and He is our prize
Drawn to redemption by the grace in his eyes
If grace is an ocean, we're all sinking[10]

Undignified celebration. Unlooked for exaltation and glory. A love so lavishly poured out, life-breathing—undeserved, yet so desperately needed and so latched upon for life. How He loves us!

WHAT IT MEANT TO GOMER

So heaven meets earth like a sloppy wet kiss
And my heart turns violently inside of my chest
I don't have time to maintain these regrets
when I think about the way
He loves us oh
Oh how He loves us...[11]

---

[10] John Mark McMillan. *The Medicine.* Integrity Music – 48152. 2010. Compact Disc.

[11] Ibid.

In Gomer's world, she was not even worthy to be a prostitute. She was up for sale. If you're feeling judgment toward Gomer rather than compassion, you will miss everything that's been said. The unrestrained love of Hosea for Gomer was ultimate.

That kind of love puts the human heart out of its reckoning. It is simply overwhelmed, pounding hard in the chest. A love that pursues like that doesn't give you the chance to stay in regret. If anyone had opportunity for that, it was Gomer. Gomer was brought back to everything she could have had all those years before. But a true fervent love—one that chases, surrounds, envelopes—makes no room for regret. The past is forgotten in the glory and security of the embraced *now*.

He loves us
Oh how He loves us
He loves us
how He loves us oh![12]

---

[12] John Mark McMillan. *The Medicine*. Integrity Music – 48152. 2010. Compact Disc.

CHAPTER SIX

LONG LAY THE WORLD

And so, for Hosea, the journey has a happy ending. Gomer is home—redeemed. Israel—the world—*mankind*—is still cheating. For Yahweh, nothing has changed. Barely ten years pass from the ending of Hosea's ministry when everything he, Amos, and Micah had forewarned the Northern Kingdom about had come to pass. In 722 BC, the Assyrians decimate the Northern ten tribes of Israel. Just as Hosea had deprived Gomer of any further provision during her time with her lover, leaving her to experience for a while the pains of enslavement, so Yahweh now withdraws His protection from the nation. Its people were now driven from their ancestral homes, forced into slavery and destitution in a foreign land.

Still to come were those prophets who would confirm Hosea's message to the Jewish people. Zephaniah, Habakkuk, Jeremiah—all of them delivering similar messages of impending doom and—a future with a surprising hope. Eventually, even the Southern Kingdom of Judah and Benjamin would fall to the Babylonians in 586 BC. Like their Northern counterparts, they had come to depend on the Baals, other foreign leaders, and financial schemes to be to them what Yahweh had covenanted with them to be.

From 605 BC to 534 BC, both Daniel and Ezekiel would continue to speak of the surprise that awaited a people in exile. The message of the coming gift would intensify with the passing years, as the Jewish people were finally permitted to return home from Babylon in 539 BC. Haggai, Zechariah, and Malachi are literally the prophets of Christmas Eve. They are the last to extrapolate and declare to a people whose spiritual minds remained deaf to a coming hope. A hope that was *alluring* their hearts back to Yahweh.

IT WASN'T JUST ISRAEL

By the way, it's important to point out that it wasn't just Israel who had cheated. From the beginning, it was all of mankind that had become estranged from Yahweh. The adultery of Israel is especially egregious because of the special covenant relationship Yahweh had initiated with them. **However, it was never supposed to be just about them. Yahweh was showing Himself to Israel so that Israel, in turn, would show Yahweh to the world.** They had failed Him miserably. The coming surprise, however, would remedy that.

EVERYBODY ELSE

What estranged evil was everybody else wrapped up in during the 600's BC? The Far Eastern peoples, including the Chinese, were giving credit to animistic spirits—ancestors who had passed. Some deities had names, others were more like unseen forces. In India, they were engaging Brahma, Vishnu, Shiva and even Kali. Kali, like Moloch, was and is an extreme evil, involving human sacrifice. In Grecian culture, the sex, finance, and war gods were epically depended upon. You've heard of them: Zeus, Athena, Apollo, Hermes, and Aphrodite, to name a few. The Assyrians and Babylonians, both sharing similar religious underpinnings, were trusting Ishtar and Marduk. A few, like Nebuchadnezzar, were brash enough to have the world worship and trust their human persons for provision. The Anglo-Saxons had a deity to credit for just about everything—horses, sunshine, rain, harvest, etc. The Incan people were both fawning and shaking in fear to pacify their chosen providers and protectors. There was Inti (god of the sun), Mama Quilla (goddess of the moon), Pachamama (goddess of the earth), and Viracocha (the first god to create the earth). Last, but certainly not least, was Supay (god of death). They look rather harmless when you're riding the Mexico ride in Disney's Epcot, but again, like the evils of Moloch and Kali, the Incans were no strangers to human sacrifice intended to incite provision of need. Their North American counterparts, due, in part, to tribalism, pandered to too many deities to account for here in this writing. Much of Africa, not unlike today, was steeped in animism, but was highly susceptible to the introduction of Phoenician and Egyptian influences.

Obviously, this list is grossly incomplete. If you have a bit of time for pursuing the question of *why does evil linger where it does?,* I would encourage you to pick up George Otis Jr.'s *The Twilight Labyrinth.* There, you will receive an education behind the veil of the world's religious systems. But for now, I hope you get the point. While Israel may have committed covenantal adultery, the world has been fornicating with foreign lovers all along. The heart of Yahweh is just as broken for one as He is the other. Why?

A COMMON PLIGHT

Sin carries real pain. You should probably underline that. This book began by discussing the foundational issue of real need. In particular, time was spent considering the perversion of need and want in view of the real-lived hurt it can bring. When we take into view the world religious systems, we find a world starving for the basic necessities of physical and metaphysical life. When you take the time to study each in view and understanding of the Mosaic laws that really do protect and provide for the individual, you find systems of belief that ignore and trample warnings meant to put food on the table, clothes on the body, souls (emotion, will, and intellects) kept secure. Personal ethos and cosmos kept right-sized in a world that demands community.

On a practical level, as Yahweh is yearning to bring His creation back into His Fathering and Mothering heart, these infidelities propagate a world in which slavery is an accepted norm: women are little more than property to be used, social class has distinctions that pass with impunity from generation to generation, rampant disease from hygiene and sexual perversion, human sacrifice, financial systems that punish the poor as a reward to the rich, lands laid waste for lack of wisdom, people groups that attack and slay others because of race all because of a coveting spirit that fails to rest contentedly in what they were given. Again, the ailments of the times can be extended beyond count. All of it: hurt. All of it: pain. All of it: stemming from hearts that seek to meet need from the places that only deepen it.

In 1847, Placide Cappeau de Roqueaure of France penned a poem at the request of His parish priest. It would eventually be set to music becoming a staple of church Christmas hymnody. You know it as *Oh Holy Night.* In it, he writes a line that captures the plight of not only Israel, but of all mankind, that only intensified from those years when the promise of redemption was made in Hosea. Roqueaure's words ring true in light of a world awaiting the surprise that would come: ***Long lay the world in sin and error pining.***[13]

A rescue from a deep fornication was desperately needed. With every passing year, lurching decade, slow-drifting century, the cries would become louder as the hurts deepened and the wounds accumulated.

O Come, O Come Emmanuel.

---

[13] *Oh Holy Night.* **1847** - 1847 w. Placide Clappeau, French, English translation John S. Dwight, m. Adolphe C. Adam.

CHAPTER SEVEN

UNFUCKING THE WORLD

Years before the discovery of my new favorite Christmas song, I was blessed to share a few days with my mentor, friend, and former professor. Larry Mitchell is simply one of my most favorite people on the planet. Few are more passionate about *living like Jesus* in community with others. I had invited him to join me on a discipleship retreat in Pass-a-grille, Florida. Significant things had been and were still happening that week. It was a sweet time made even better by his presence.

As things worked out, Larry needed to get to the airport a day early to make his way back to Indianapolis. Having reached the check-in curb and preparing to part, he pulled me close and drew my eyes to his saying, "I want to share something with you. It's a secret handshake I share with my son." Larry confessed that they had gotten the idea from Viggo Mortensen (Aragorn, for *The Lord of the Rings* fans reading). We were to engage in a Roman-type handshake, grasping one another's right forearms, embracing closely with the left arm and whispering into each other's ears..."*Unfuck the world.*"

It was one of those moments where I would have liked to have been Larry staring into my widening eyes. I love Larry...not disappointing him and not letting him down is pretty close to a non-negotiable for me. However, this was hard. I wanted to say to him, "*Larry... Uhh... I'm a preacher from North Carolina. It's a Southern state, you know. We don't say things like that. That's a dirty word, Larry!*"

Keeping those thoughts to myself, I weakly participated in the initial handshake, saying *unfuck* as inaudibly and unrecognizably as possible.

Years later, as Christmas neared and the Hosea story began to merge in my spirit with *How He Loves,* I began to rethink the *handshake.* Maybe it wasn't all that inappropriate after all. I needed to do some research on the origins and original meanings of the "word." Google didn't disappoint.

Fuck, as you may discover—if you attempt to uncover its origins for yourself—is quite the mystery. In all likelihood, it is a word for which the answer may never truly be known. However, one legend caught my attention. I make no claims to assert that this opinion is the correct one. Again, I would suggest that, until archeological evidence proves conclusive, it's simply a word that has something to do with sex. Beyond that, everything is speculation. The legend I discovered, however, has become rather popular. It kind of has two versions that may be related or not.

The first is a bit more salacious, involving the subjugation of Scottish husbands and fathers. Legend has it that the King of England granted permission to his nobles to take the wives and daughters of Scotsmen in for the night to fornicate with them as a way of humiliating and demonstrating his authority over the people. As fornication was, in point of fact, forbidden by law in England, the King drafted a document entitled ***Fornication Under Consent of the King***, thereby temporarily absolving the King's loyal fornicators. Over time, the document simply became known as a *"fuck."*

The alternate version of the story links the *fuck document* to the need for the English peoples to procreate quickly due to the massive death tolls associated with the plague. Some have gone so far as to link the events suggesting the commonality of the practice at that time.

Again, is it the true origin of the word? I don't know. Be that as it may, it gave me a way to say *"the word"* without pang of conscience. I still can't, and feel I shouldn't use the word in jest or for the God-ordained physical relationship I have with my wife. It is far above that...whatever its origin. However, in view of Hosea's story, and in view of Yahweh's demonstrated and written feelings about the adultery and fornication of His creation, I could certainly not only say, but engage in the *Un***Fornication** of the world **Under Consent** of the **King.**

When I read Hosea and the Christmas story, I find that is exactly what Jesus was coming to do. He was coming to radically *unfuck* the world. For indeed, it had become fubar (you can look that one up for yourself).

AND STILL…

For 700+ years—from Hosea's *alluring* Gomer—Yahweh continues to whisper over a world that is still fornicating—still mired in adultery—still prostituting itself for gain: *I've got a secret.*

Of those Prophets that would give the messages of Yahweh to Israel, Malachi would be the last to speak. Four hundred years would pass before Yahweh would break his long silence. In the meantime, *normal*, as they would prefer it, would not come to the Jewish people.

Even before Malachi silenced his voice, the Jewish people were coming back to the land. However, it wasn't the same. The Temple had been rebuilt, but it did not compare to the glory of the one Solomon had constructed. They were in their own land, but they did not rule themselves. The Babylonian rulers would be overcome by Alexander the Great. The Grecian rulers would eventually be supplanted by Roman proxy rulers.

The arrival of the Herodian Dynasty remains to this day a black period in Jewish history. The Jewish people knew their heritage and laws quite well. Only a descendant of David could claim the throne. The Romans could care less. They needed a puppet to keep the rabble in line. Herod was a particular offense to the Jews. He was neither of David's line nor fully

Jewish. His lust for power is clearly demonstrated in Matthew 2:16-23.

If you remember the Christmas story, the *wise men*—magi, who were passing through Jerusalem on their way to the Christ child, were brought to speak with Herod. They had seen through his intentions then. Herod made them known not long after. Fearing the security of his own reign, he dared to kill God. *Hear that!* What Messiah was prophesied to be was no secret. That's precisely who the wise men were looking for. It was the obsession of the God-fearing priest at that time. This Messiah was Emmanuel—God with us—*Yahweh with us*, and Herod knew it and still dared to kill him. On his command, every firstborn male, two years old and under, living in the vicinity of Bethlehem, was slaughtered.

As the Apostle Matthew remembered, Jeremiah had prophesied of this day, writing:

A voice was heard in Ramah,
Weeping and great mourning,
Rachel weeping for her children;
And she refused to be comforted,
Because they were no more.

Jeremiah 31:15 // Matthew 2:18

Israel remained a people under the thumb of an empire with fickle authorities that had zero appreciation for the value of life. Anything that was owned, was done so precariously, with no guarantees. The exile had taught this people to become zealous over the law, yet Herod had little compunction concerning the luxuries of Hellenistic life.

Hellenistic worship was nothing short of sex-charged degradation. To counter-balance this, the Pharisees who had arisen almost in response to the invasion of Greek religious culture around them made laws to keep their Jewish people from breaking the Mosaic laws. They were ruthless in their pursuit and hypocritical in their practice. Jesus would later be most harsh with these men, calling them *vipers* and *white-washed tombs.* (Matthew 12:34 and 23:27)

The rest of the world remained entrenched, placating their demonic deities, attempting to be happy with the scraps they believed were thrown their way. It is fascinating to observe the world-over that the relationships that exist between the pagan gods and their subjects are never an altruistic kind of giving love. They are pernicious, vindictive, fickle, tricky, vaguely benevolent when it suits them—but never condescending to *authentic relationship*. Only Yahweh offers such an unthinkable grace.

OH COME, OH COME…

Increasingly, the cry of the Jewish people would become,

O come, O come, Emmanuel
And ransom captive Israel
That mourns in lonely exile here

Until the Son of God appear[14]

When Messiah appeared, the unfucking of the world would begin. Again Roqueaure penned it well:

Chains shall He break for the slave is our brother
And in His name all oppression shall cease[15]

I've got a surprise for you, beloved. I'm coming. I'm coming for you. And when I get there, I'm going to do something for you beyond the scope of your imagination. I have an unlooked for gift to give. "A gift to give that you don't know how to expect." I'm coming. Wait for it. I'm coming. All that causes the hurt, I am about to un-do. All who have cheated on Me and given themselves to other things—I'm about to woo you back, and you'll never guess how I'm going to do it. I'm coming.

---

[14] *Oh Come Emmanuel.* 1850s - w. translation John Mason Neale, Henry Sloane Coffin, m. French Hymn, 1400s.

[15] *Oh Holy Night.* **1847** - 1847 w. Placide Clappeau, French, English translation John S. Dwight, m. Adolphe C. Adam.

CHAPTER EIGHT

CHRISTMAS EVE

In all of the 365 days of the live-long year, is there a longer night for children than the 358th one?! It's absolutely brutal. I make no apologies for being the son of a middle of the middle class. We were blessed. My parents loved each other, and they loved us. We weren't given cars, motorcycles, the latest video games...but we did receive much, and for every last bit of it, I am humbled and grateful.

Not only was I unspeakably blessed with amazing parents, I was raised in a very special area of the country. The Triad of North Carolina—Winston-Salem, Greensboro, and High Point—is a relatively affluent area where things are nice and the cost of living is reasonably low for the things we enjoy and have. These cities and their shopping centers knew how to decorate well. The Hanes Mall boasted a poinsettia Christmas tree that stood over three stories high. All along its concourse were animatronic elf displays that lit the fires of our imaginations. When I walked these halls, I truly felt as if I had come to the North Pole itself. The traditional trip to have my picture taken with Santa all but made it so.

Few things captured my attention more than the Christmas lights that adorned the houses up and down our community roads. The color of Christmas was everywhere. These were the days preceding ABC Family's 25 days of Christmas. The Christmas specials were just that—*special.* The TV guide (sorry millennials and post-millennials), an actual smallish-sized paper publication announcing programming every two weeks was essential to know when the *claymations* would air.

And of course, there were the Christmas foods. Moravian Christmas cookies, Moravian sugar bread, Christmas sugar cookies that we would bake and decorate ourselves! Sausage balls, hot apple cider and wassail, gingerbread houses, candy canes, peppermint teas, Christmas hams, egg nog, and more!

Everything about Thanksgiving to December 24th in the marketing and family worlds led up to this day!

Most North American families have specific traditions for Christmas Eve that nearly rival *the* day that follows. Our family was no different. As a child, it included an hour and a half road trip to Rockingham, NC to have dinner, open gifts, and play hard with the cousins. My brother and I loved that trip. We loved the wreaths hung from the street lights in Thomasville, NC. We knew exactly where the lit houses were located as they served as our landmarks for how close we were getting to my grandparents' home.

While we loved the gifts that were given, my memories are most rapt from the anticipation we shared with our cousins. *"Do you know what you're going to get?" "No, I know what I asked for, but I don't have a clue." "Hey...I snuck into the back space of my mom's closet....shhhhhh....." "I'm getting an Intellivision"..."What?!" Are you serious?!?"* (I apologize, once again, millennial and younger friends—the Intellivision came on the heels of the Atari 2600...It didn't last very long.) On and on we would go, making our best guesses, wishing the night away to the big reveal that would come for each of us in the morning.

On the ride home, my mom would stoke our anticipation, pointing at every blinking light in the sky. "*Do you think it could be him?"* My Dad seemed to enjoy these games. "*I bet it is boys—that ain't no plane; that's a sleigh!"* My dad was a heavy maintenance mechanic for Piedmont Airlines, so of course, he would know.

Once home, it was time for bed. After the Christmas cookies were set out for Santa, we were in our beds for a tradition I still hold with the fondest of memories. MY MOM IS THE BEST *Night before Christmas* reader EVER!!! When she read Moore's poem, Santa and his reindeer came alive. And then the lights went out, *and we waited.*

10 o'clock turned to 10:15pm—10:15 to 10:27—10:27 to 10:35—10:35 to 10:48—and on and on it went. Eyes would close only to open moments later to see the long night was still before me. 2 a.m. would turn 2:13 a.m. It seemed the night would never pass. But,

at last—I could never tell when—my eyes would close for good, drifting into dreams fueled by sights and sounds of a season trafficking in sensory overload. And then—

ALL TIMES SOON

C.S. Lewis's Lucy was anxious to know when she would see Aslan again. Would it be soon? The great lion responded by saying, "*I call all times soon.*"[16]

The greatest surprises are nearly always met with the greatest *waits*. Please don't miss that. I think on the infinite Yahweh's timeline, great waits are not necessarily long waits. It is the degree of anticipation that determines the *feelings* of the wait. The Prophets wrote as if it would all happen tomorrow. But Yahweh calls *all times soon.* The *Christmas Eve* of Israel and mankind would turn out to be a thirty-three year long night. Meanwhile, the prophetic voices had gone dark. Only the whispers of the coming surprise were left—so we waited.

The priests and wise men gathered throughout the seasons pondering *who it would be—when it might be*—hoping someone might know what they did not. Is He coming now? Could this be the event? Could this be the catalyst that brings Messiah's return? The world waited and waited, and then—on a day that was passing like all of the long ones before it, the four

---

[16] C.S. Lewis. *Chronicles of Narnia,* (New York, NY: Harper Collins, 2001), 499.

hundred year silence was broken. No one—*no one* —expected it.

HEY ZACHARIAS//HEY MARY//TWAS THE NIGHT BEFORE CHRISTMAS

According to Luke chapter one, it was Zacharias' turn to burn incense in the *Holy Place* just outside of the *Holy of Holies.* Luke has some nice things to say about Zacharias. When we're introduced to the Pharisees, Sadducees, and scribes thirty years later, we catch a glimpse of how different he was. Of both Zacharias and Elizabeth, his wife, Luke writes, "They were both righteous in the sight of God, walking blamelessly in all the commandments and requirements of the Lord." (Luke 1:6)

Concerning the incense, it was a solemn task that was taken with utmost attention to detail. While the rituals pertaining to duties inside the *Holy of Holies* carried life and death consequences for the High Priest, the Holy Place remained a very big deal in its own right. It was something which was commanded to be done twice a day in perpetuity (Exodus 30:1-10). When Zacharias entered the room known as the Holy Place that morning, according to the ritual laws, he entered alone—or at least thought he had.

Keeping in mind that nothing prophetically significant has been spoken in nearly four hundred years, what happened next is nearly unbelievable on the scale of...: expecting the sixteen-seed *play-in* team of the NCAA tournament to win the national championship by blowing out Duke after having handily dispatched

North Carolina and Kentucky. Possibly more relevant, would have been to expect in 1992, that Donald Trump would someday be the President of the United States. In either case, you just wouldn't have expected it—ever!

Can you imagine Zacharias' utter surprise that morning when he walked into the Holy Place to perform this solemn duty, to find someone standing by the incense altar! Not just anyone—but an angel **of the Lord**. Verse twelve says that, "Zacharias was troubled when he saw the angel, and fear gripped him." Of course it did! Zacharias was supposed to be the only one in there. Foul-ups like that could cost you your **life**.

Immediately, the angel sought to comfort Zacharias, calming his fear. What the angel had to say would place Zacharias at the forefront of everything the Prophets had spoken. It would test his faith as it did Abraham's. Incidentally, this wasn't just *any* angel. Not that it would have diminished the message. However, this one carried a rather unique and singular weight. *It was Gabriel.* Not the Gabriel that lore and pop culture movies have commonly referenced. This is the Gabriel who stood in the presence of Yahweh! That alone may have been enough to explain Zacharias' initial fear. Moses was exposed to the *back side* of Yahweh's glory and was made to wear a bag over his head to calm the fears of the people, such was the effect of being in Yahweh's presence. Gabriel had spent the better part of eternity up until then *standing in His presence.*

When *Gabriel* personally delivers the message—*it's really, really big!*

The test of faith? Like Abraham and Sarah, Zacharias and Elizabeth had been childless and were now well past the age of having children. Gabriel gave them the unthinkable news that they would be the true biological parents of the child that would be the *Elijah* all of Israel had been waiting for (v.17). This child would announce the direct arrival of the long—very long—awaited Messiah. They were to name him John, and in lieu of that, the remainder of Zacharias' days were to be lived in joy. Again, like Abraham, he couldn't help himself. He needed confirmation to gird his faith.

Gabriel gave it to him in what had to be a rather unwelcoming way. He caused Zacharias to become mute until John's birth (vs. 18-20). AHHHH! Really! *Can you imagine having just received the greatest news to have ever been uttered to the world and not be able to share or talk about it?* Even so, when he finally emerged from the Holy Place, everyone knew something significant had happened. Zacharias was obviously beside himself. Making signs and trying to communicate in any way that he could were all rather useless in that moment. Weeks, maybe a month later, Elizabeth got it full on (vs. 24-25). Something completely *other* was in motion.

MARY'S TURN

In a remarkable turn of events, Mary, the cousin of Elizabeth, was about to get a visit of her own. As far as message deliveries go, this one was the highest priority delivery of all time. Again, none other than Gabriel had drawn the assignment. (v. 26)

If you're thinking Mary is arbitrarily chosen, think again. Things set in motion from the days of Amos, Hosea, Micah, Isaiah, and Zechariah now burst forth into fruition. The Messiah was to sit on the throne of David. Yet only a descendant of David could do so. Both Mary and Joseph qualify. Mary comes of the *bloodline* of David, while Joseph comes of the *kingly* line of David. (Matthew 1:1-16 & Luke 3:23-31) Strategic things are happening when and how they were least expected.

From the looks of things, it was a house visit. Hear for yourself what he has to say, "Greetings, favored one! The Lord is with you." (v.28) If you're wondering, males—as Gabriel seems to present himself—don't speak to Jewish girls like this. Yes, I know, he's an Angel—Gabriel, no less. Even so, Mary's hesitancy at the greeting is completely understandable. He continues:

> "Do not be afraid, Mary; for you have found favor with God. And behold, you will conceive in your womb and bear a son, and you shall name Him Jesus. He will be great and will be called the Son of the Most High; and the Lord God will give Him the throne of His father David; and He will reign over the house of Jacob forever, and His kingdom will have no end." Luke 1:30-33

There, in that very private and unexpected moment, the announcement that every God-fearing Jew had waited to hear from the days of the Prophets, hundreds and hundreds of years before, was broken open to a young girl. A royal family reduced to commonality among its people received the news when and where none could expect anything to come of it.

Mary's next question is beautiful. It's not a *lack of faith* question so much as a question of *wonder.* Just how exactly does a virgin get pregnant? Gabriel has the answer and more:

"The Holy Spirit will come upon you, and the power of the Most High will overshadow you; and for that reason the holy Child shall be called the Son of God. And behold, even your relative Elizabeth has also conceived a son in her old age; and she who was called barren is now in her sixth month. For nothing will be impossible with God."

Luke 1:35-36

After all we've discussed regarding *bitter cups* and the way things were expected to happen in Jewish culture, everything about this is beyond the pale. If you can believe it, this isn't even the greatest part of the surprise that Yahweh has coming! But certainly, it is surprising enough. Poor Joseph! Blessed Joseph! *Oh my, Joseph!* No worries—if you've read the story, you know Yahweh provides him with a dream that puts Joseph in the very exclusive *know.* (Matthew 1:20-21) What's more, **he tells Joseph His intention to *unfuck the world* (whether he realizes it or not!)—by telling him, "...He will save His people from their sins."** (Matthew 1:21)

Perhaps my favorite part of this whole passage is Mary's response. A mentor and the man who officiated my wedding shared an insight during a youth camp I have never forgotten. After a conversation taking a mere 50.2 seconds, that could potentially shatter her life (unwed mothers had extremely poor prospects in those days!)—Mary *immediately* replies, “Behold, the bondslave of the Lord; may it be done to me according to your word.” (Luke 1:38) Wow! No Moses or Gideon is she! Including Esther, perhaps Mary is the bravest young lady to have ever walked the planet.

Welcome to Christmas Eve—a thirty-three and a half year adventure.

CHAPTER NINE

SILENT NIGHT?

It's certainly one of my favorite Christmas hymns. David Crowder's live rendition may be my most-listened to at present. It has a way of laying my heart at rest when the anxieties of the season begin to press. Quite frankly, it seems to serve as a kind of therapy song for me at that time of year. Mary and Joseph, however, had no such song. They had the real historical days to trudge—and they were anything but silent.

Luke 2:1 opens, "Now in those days a decree went out from Caesar Augustus, that a census be taken of all the inhabited earth...And everyone was on his way to register for the census, each to his own city." For Joseph and his very pregnant wife, that meant a road trip—a journey that would take them from Nazareth to Bethlehem. Our ability to travel in the 21st century obscures the chaos of these events—especially for a young couple preparing to birth their first child into the world.

If you have a Bible map handy, you'll notice Nazareth is very much North of Bethlehem. There are many factors to consider concerning this trip. While it was geographically a trip down, it was a journey up. The terrain was mountainous. There is some question regarding the donkey we see on the post cards. Did they have one or didn't they? As Joseph was a carpenter and would likely need to find work in Bethlehem, he may have needed to bring some tools of the trade. They are walking and will need to eat. Food stocks, even if relatively minimal, would be needed. Other personal belongings might also be expected. *If* a donkey made the trip, while making their burdens lighter, it would not have necessarily made it faster. Donkeys often seem to have minds of their own.

While the census is disruption to life, the journey still rests somewhat in the flow of life-living as it would have for all of us. To think they walked out of the door with only the clothes on their back for a four to ten day walk, and days to be spent in Bethlehem undetermined, is unrealistic. Like people do, preparations would have been made.

Yes, if you're wondering, given the roads they had to take and covering an estimated distance of eighty plus miles, four to ten days was what you could expect for that journey. For a Nazarene going to Bethlehem, it could be a risky one. Rogue thieves and bandits were a common menace on these roads. With no helicopters, radios, cell phone tracking—it was easy for criminals to take advantage. There was a rather inconvenient route choice to make as well. The fastest route would walk them through Samaria.

The Samaritans and Jews weren't on the friendliest of terms. The Jews, having an upturned nose toward the Samaritans, had managed to offend them to the point of frequent contention. It also meant making your way through a very busy and very crowded Jerusalem overrun with Roman soldiers and the typical opportunists large cities attract.

So, did they travel alone? Probably not. There was safety in numbers. Could they have dared it alone? Sure, but why? Remember, everyone has to go back to their ancestral homes to register. Finding a party headed in their general direction wouldn't have been hard. With Mary approaching *blast off,* it is highly unlikely that he would make the trip without some ladies to serve as midwives should the need arise.

Some have asked the question regarding their accommodations for the journey. Where did they sleep? As Jewish people had a custom of housing passersby, it is likely they had a few evenings in welcoming homes and a few more camped out with their traveling companions. Regardless, these were considerations that would not be made lightly. If you were availing yourself of hospitality, it needed to be done without running up a debt. If you were camped out, somebody likely needed to be up and watching. Again, roaming bandits would take advantage where they could.

There were also the political thunderclouds that perpetually hung over the land in these days. Herod the Great, evil though he may have been, had seemingly provided some level of livable stability in the land. But it was precarious, as the demand for a census makes clear. The paranoid Herod had become dark in his old age. No one was safe, not even his sons. Who would rule in his stead after his death? It mattered. The wrong man might bring the wrath of Rome down on all of them. Even so, there were those Jewish zealots that would have Herod and Rome gone *now*! What kind of mess could they get the average Jewish citizen into, if in their zeal and haste, they engaged in violence at the wrong time or assassinated the wrong Roman? It was a nervous time to to be alive in Palestine.

What does it all mean? *Upheaval.* Villains—who would take advantage of the people most at risk during times like these. Financial burden—road trips always are—even today. Physical challenge. In two words **Stress—Anxiety.** These were not quiet days or times.

WHAT CHILD IS THIS

What Child is this
Who laid to rest
On Mary's lap is sleeping?
Whom Angels greet with anthems sweet,
While shepherds watch are keeping...[17]

And so the night came....The trek from Nazareth had been completed. I don't want to crash any cherished Nativity scenes you may hold in your head, but the evening may have been way different than pop culture

---

[17] *What Child Is This.* 1865 - 1865 - William C. Dix, m. 16th Century English Traditional.

has made it. We like to think of Joseph arriving in town at the nick of time, beating on "Inn" doors desperately looking for a place for Mary to give birth. The context of the passage however fails to picture that kind of urgency.

From the looks of things, Joseph and Mary arrived without event and were waiting for "the day." No doubt, it didn't take long and may not have been the panic-stricken ordeal we've pictured. As for *no room in the inn* (v.7), it was not a matter of heartless innkeepers, but rather, the floor plan of Jewish homes. A guest room—called an inn— would have been typical. One of two scenarios were likely: the guest room was simply too small to contain both Mary and the midwives that would have assisted her. Or, remembering that there would have been a large influx of people due to the census, the guest room may have been full. Chances are, Joseph and Mary were crashing with distant family or even family friends. If this was the case, it simply meant Joseph and Mary were staying in the part of the home that housed the livestock. Unlike North American farm properties, Jewish homes were designed to house the animals they owned for basic needs. To lay him in a manger would have worked in lieu of the floor Mary and Joseph were most likely using inside the house.

So, what's so special about that? Uhhh...*GOD* WAS BEING BORN! Yes, the lowly image of a neglected family in need is touching, but completely unnecessary for the grandeur of this moment. Jesus could have been born in Rome, wrapped in royal linens, laid in a crib of pure gold studded with diamonds. The whole world could have lined up outside the door bringing the value of all they owned to lay at his feet and it still would have been a slum hole in comparison to what He had temporarily left behind.

YAHWEH GOES PUBLIC

Demonstrating the big deal of it all, you need to read a few verses more. Luke 2:8 gives the immediate context of the birth of Emmanuel. Again, it comes in ways the wise and self-important would never guess. Does Yahweh announce the birth of His Son to Herod? To the High Priest of the Jewish temple? To Caesar Augustus? *Nope*. He announces it to shepherds in a nearby field—*and it's quite the production.*

Luke 2:9 recounts the event, "And an angel of the Lord suddenly stood before them, and the glory of the Lord shone around them; and they were terribly frightened." Often in the scriptures when Angels—messengers from Yahweh—appear before men, they seem to do so in ways that don't completely freak them out—not always, but usually. *Not this time.* These angels are in true form with the brightness of Yahweh beaming in blinding light from their beings. *Of course* the shepherds are terrified.

Listen to the announcement they make for all of mankind:

"Do not be afraid; for behold, I bring you good news of great joy which will be for all the people; for today in the city of David there has been born for you a Savior, who is

Christ the Lord. This will be a sign for you: you will find a baby wrapped in cloths and lying in a manger."

Luke 2:10-12

That alone is a bit much to take in. In the moment, you can't. It requires the whole of the story to that point in the saga of man and Yahweh to even begin to appreciate it. Even then, I can't.

It is *other.*

God entered earth via a birthday suit to walk among us?!?!?

Not just to walk, but to *save.*

To *unfuck* the world.

Anyone living in those times, or anyone living in ours should instinctively know what that announcement could mean in a world of hurt—degradation—slavery—disease—famine—wars—crime—sin.

The angels did.

"And suddenly there appeared with the angel a multitude of the heavenly host, praising God and saying, 'Glory to God in the highest, and on earth peace among men with whom He is pleased.'" Luke 2:13-14

Something foundationally existence-altering was in motion—**and all of heaven knew it**.

The *surprise*—the *real gift* was coming....

THE OLD WRAPPING TRICK

But there was more. Have you ever received or given the gift that took forever to unwrap? You know—the practical joke kind of wrapping perhaps. You remove the first layer of paper only to find another and another. You get to the box, only to find it is in another box and quite possibly another wrapped in paper yet again! **The Christmas story taken in full context is kind of like that.** Or maybe it's the kind of gift that came in a bag with lots of tissue paper. You bring out one item only for the giver to say, "*keep looking—there's more.*" Yes, Jesus is born, and it is a beautiful thing to unwrap—but the real surprise is still waiting.

But first, a Christmas offering from my eldest, Tsion Scott Reid:

NOT SO SILENT

Who knew the star from afar would cause such a roar.
That silent night, yes, it was silent for over 100 thousand nights.
We were full of fear, and geared wrong all those years.
Built right, then corrupted; life, it erupted, He conducted, created from abstraction, cleared everything of distraction, what a reaction, not just a religious action, not a fraction, or a retraction but a regeneration of all generations, the Christ has come on this not so silent night.[18]

Tsion Reid

---

[18] Tsion Scott Reid. *Not So Silent...* , unpublished, Winston-Salem, NC, 2017.

CHAPTER TEN

UNFUCKING THE WORLD INDEED

Outside of a visit to Jerusalem, and a few days of panic for Mary and Joseph before a young Jesus would be found at the Temple, the next thirty years are rather uneventful. All of that changes when Jesus performs His first public miracle at Cana, turning water into wine (Jn. 2:1-11). From that moment on, the thought and traditions of man would be fatally countered.

When we follow Jesus through the gospel accounts, the Man who walks those experiences is undeniably a Man set apart from history. In a world that subjugated women, He publicly honored and valued them. In a world of radicals sowing discord and violence, He gave respect to authority, even when His teaching undercut their worldviews and systems. He was a teacher, a Rabbi, that was open to all—not just the socially gifted. Finance had no power over Him. He moved at will and blessed where He would. Social classes did not affect Him in the least—Pilate could hold life and death over His head, and still Jesus could stand before Him unimpressed and immovable.

He was tender of heart like none the world had ever seen. John, a personal companion and disciple said of Jesus, "And there are also many other things which Jesus did, which if they were written in detail, I suppose that even the world itself would not contain the books that would be written." (Jn 21:25) The gospels vaguely paint that picture. Lepers, cripples, the blind, the deaf, the insane, the demon-possessed—all found healing when they encountered Jesus. Be they Jew, Samaritan, Roman—man, woman, or child—He embraced them all. Whether they were community whores, financial conmen, proud upperclass, enemies, religious elite (provided they had the humility to listen to Him)...they all found a place at the table.

We say this is special and revolutionary for its time. Let's be honest, it's revolutionary for *our* time. In America, we love to give lip service to our cares and concerns for the poor among us. Laughably, those who champion the most from the political spheres fence themselves off and deride the peasant masses in their private circles the most. They toss out the government's money (which is really the people's money) and expect it to be enough. Jesus didn't operate that way. Jesus, more than not, moved by personal touch—not self-serving campaign slogans (something for modern day politicians to ponder).

To that end, it might be good to be reminded of the injustices Jesus confronted. Most all of it was reserved for the religious elite of His own people. He accused them of taking advantage of widows and the poor, praying publicly for show and personal attention, for calling hell down on minor matters while they dishonored their own parents. He actually said of them, "Woe to you, scribes and Pharisees, hypocrites! For you are like whitewashed tombs which on the outside appear beautiful, but inside they are full of dead men's bones and all uncleanness." (Matthew 23:27)

JESUS' LIFE-LIVING WAS DIFFERENT

That Jesus was different is attested to throughout the world's major religions. While radical Muslims have no love for Christians, they hold a deep respect for Jesus. In fact, they consider Him one of the greatest, if not the greatest prophet of Islam. Yes, they ultimately miss Him by failing to take Him for what He Himself claimed to be—God—but their respect of His teachings is undeniable.

The Hindus reverence Jesus as a great teacher as well—even a god—*little g*. However, like the Muslims, they deny His true identity. Buddhist and New Age practitioners alike espouse His moral teachings. No other human to have walked the earth has garnered the respect and attention of Jesus. Oddly enough, even among the followers of pagan gods and empty religious systems with whom mankind continues to spiritually fornicate, Jesus is admired.

For any tempted to respect Jesus in these ways, I believe C.S. Lewis spoke with founded reason on the matter:

> I am trying here to prevent anyone saying the really foolish thing that people often say about Him: I'm ready to accept Jesus as a great moral teacher, but I don't accept his claim to be God. That is the one thing we must not say. A man who was merely a man and said the sort of things Jesus said would not be a great moral teacher. He would either be a lunatic — on the level with the man who says he is a poached egg — or else he would be the Devil of Hell. You must make your choice. Either this man was, and is, the Son of God, or else a madman or something worse. You can shut him up for a fool, you can spit at him and kill him as a demon or you can fall at his feet and call him Lord and God, but let us not come with any patronizing nonsense about his being a great human teacher. He has not left that open to us. He did not intend to.[19]

So what did Jesus intend to do?

UNFUCK THE WORLD

Thirty-three and a half years later, Jesus shocks the world at the cross. It wasn't to come and do good things. He does those things to show us what an *unfornicating* of the world would look like—what *unfornicators* would someday, in the very near future, be about. Healing the hurts, holding the lonely, living like rivers among need. But the penultimate goal—the surprise—is THE CROSS.

And what is the cross? Hosea's story should have told you——————————————

---

[19] C.S. Lewis. *Mere Christianity* (SanFrancisco, CA: Harper, 1952), 52.

BUY BACK

The prayer in Gethsemane, moments before the arrest that would lead to His crucifixion, should be clear enough. "'Father, if You are willing, remove this cup from Me; yet not My will, but Yours be done.'" (Luke 22:42) It was the *bitter cup* meant for an adulterating—fornicating world! ***Jesus drank the cup*—paid the price—*bought us back.*** And no one saw it coming!!! (Surprise!) *"What do ya know about that*—MERRY CHRISTMAS!!!![20]

The words of Yahweh through Hosea come back around:

---

[20] *It's A Wonderful Life.* Frank Capra, RKO Radio Pictures, 1946.

“Therefore, behold, I will allure her, bring her into the wilderness and speak kindly to her.

“Then I will give her her vineyards from there, and the valley of Achor as a door of hope. And she will sing there as in the days of her youth, as in the day when she came up from the land of Egypt.

“It will come about in that day,” declares the Lord, “That you will call Me Ishi and will no longer call Me Baali.

“For I will remove the names of the Baals from her mouth, so that they will be mentioned by their names no more.

“In that day I will also make a covenant for them With the beasts of the field, the birds of the sky And the creeping things of the ground. And I will abolish the bow, the sword and war from the land, And will make them lie down in safety.

“I will betroth you to Me forever; Yes, I will betroth you to Me in righteousness and in justice, in lovingkindness and in compassion, and I will betroth you to Me in faithfulness. Then you will know the Lord.

“It will come about in that day that I will respond,” declares the Lord. “I will respond to the heavens, and they will respond to the earth, and the earth will respond to the grain, to the new wine and to the oil,
And they will respond to Jezreel.

“I will sow her for Myself in the land. I will also have compassion on her who had not obtained compassion, and I will say to those who were not My people,‘You are My people!’ And they will say, ‘You are my God!’”

On that day, when Jesus said, "*It is finished.*" (Jn. 19:30) **The gift promised in Hosea was given.**

"When all of a sudden I'm unaware of these afflictions eclipsed by Glory (in the face of my personal fornications and adulteries of heart, mind, and deed) and I realize just how beautiful you are and how great your affections are toward me. Oh, how He loves me Oh, how He loves me."[21] (parentheses mine)

MERRY CHRISTMAS, friend.

A thrill of hope the weary world rejoices
For yonder breaks
A new and glorious morn

Fall on your knees
O hear the angel voices
O night divine
O night when Christ was born[22]

OH, HOLY NIGHT AND HALLELUJAH

In 2011, *The David Crowder Band* released a Christmas album containing *Oh Holy Night.* As it crescendoed to its end, it melted into a chorus of Hallelujahs keeping with the melody. Rarely have I felt something so appropriately done. It simply repeated

---

[21] John Mark McMillan. *The Medicine.* Integrity Music – 48152. 2010. Compact Disc.

[22] *Oh Holy Night.* **1847** - 1847 w. Placide Clappeau, French, English translation John S. Dwight, m. Adolphe C. Adam.

the soul-stealing phrase—Hallelujah, Hallelujah, Hallelujah, Hallelujah.....[23]

If you understand the meaning and the lived-action the word entails, it may help. In the Strong's NASB concordance, you will see it is two words smashed together. The front part of the word, *halal* means to be boastful and to praise—but more than that—it carries the idea of actually racing like a madman going after something—even making an idiot of yourself.[24] Much like my brother at the discovery of his Go Kart.

The second part of the word is simply the name of Yahweh—Yah. Put it together, and you begin to get the picture. Like a madman, going absolutely crazy, being undignified, praising, racing madly for Yahweh. It is the only appropriate response to a love that has pursued us like that.

Here we go a caroling—

Hallelujah – Hallelujah – Hallelujah – Hallelujah
Hallelujah – Hallelujah – Hallelujah – Hallelujah!

---

[23] David Crowder Band. *Oh For Joy.* Sparrow Records – 5099994636529, sixstepsrecords – 5099994636529, 2011, compact disc.

[24] *The Strongest NASB Exhaustive Concordance* (Grand Rapids, MI: Zondervan, 2004), 1384, 1401.

CHAPTER ELEVEN

EMMANUEL — GOD WITH US — THE GIFT THAT KEEPS ON GIVING

So, in a way, our culture, in practical living, totally seems to miss the *"twelve days of Christmas."* If you're unfamiliar with the actual dates, they run from December 25th to January 5th. Yeah, I know. Many of you have your tree packed away or tossed out to the burn pile by December 26th. Some of you more *diehard* celebrators milk it all the way to New Year's Day before you've finally had enough.

May I ask a question? Does anyone get really excited about Christmas parties that happen after December 25th? Those celebrations are usually reserved for distant family or office gatherings that couldn't be squeezed in before. Nobody really expects a lot from those. These days, they've become the gag gift parties. I've long held a desire to gift twenty dollars-worth of gift cards for a big box store with each individual card having no more than twenty-five cents on it. Yeah—deviously laughing at the moment. Post December 25th parties seem the best place to do it.

I'm only mentioning this, because there was more to the *buy back* gift—way more. And it's nothing like we've come to expect for post *big day* celebrations.

EMMANUEL

For many, the birth, crucifixion—buy back, and resurrection are everything. Indeed, I wouldn't want to say anything here that would diminish these—nor should I. Heaven grants it the most intense, unrestrained celebration ever in Revelation 5:9-14. It is *Hallelujah* over and over again! But—there's more. It involved a great deal of mystery. The Mystery? How would Yahweh be *with us?*

That had always been the principle question. For Adam and Eve, He walked with them in the cool of the day. (Gen. 3:8) Noah was given His voice and visions. (Gen. 6 & 7) Abraham was much the same with seemingly greater frequency. Moses would be altogether different. He would actually get to see the *back side* of the glory of Yahweh. (Exodus 33:20-23) In addition to that and to the great favor of Israel, His presence would travel with the Ark of the Covenant—the golden box that held the Ten Commandments, showbread, and Aaron's staff. While they journeyed in the desert after departing from Egypt, Yahweh would present Himself as a pillar of cloud by day and fire by night. He was *with them.*

When Solomon completed the first permanent Temple structure in 832 BC, it was expected that Yahweh would be with them, perpetually from that place forever. When it was destroyed by Nebuchadnezzar of Babylon in 587 BC, the question returned—How is Yahweh going to be *with us—now?* Seventy years later, they would return and the Temple would be rebuilt with great effort, and Yahweh would return to it.

When Jesus—the God-Man, comes on the scene, that Temple is still in place. But something was different in the land then. Yes, the Temple was open for worship, but Yahweh had been silent. He was with them, but He wasn't, or didn't seem to be. A prophet hadn't spoken in 400 years. At least not until John the Baptist burst on the scene announcing what oppressed Jewish citizens had been waiting and wanting to hear for generations. At last! Yahweh is going to manifest among us!

And for thirty-three and a half years—three and a half publicly—He did. Jesus was Emmanuel—*God with us*. He had demonstrated it through every form of miracle imaginable. But by all accounts, it was confusing, in terms of *how* He was going to manifest this Kingdom He spoke so frequently of. Those who *kind of knew* Him, were waiting for a show of force that would not only remove the Roman empire, but overcome it. Those who knew Him best were waiting—well—they were waiting on the same thing...Peter, John, Andrew, Phillip, Matthew, Thomas, the others—were waiting to see where their place would be in it all.

MYSTERIOUS WORDS

In view of those expectations, Jesus had begun to say some strange things that wouldn't have sounded altogether hopeful for the disciples who had followed Him most closely.

Then He took the twelve aside and said to them, "Behold, we are going up to Jerusalem, and all things which are written through the prophets about the Son of Man will be accomplished. For He will be handed over to the Gentiles, and will be mocked and mistreated and spit upon, and after they have scourged Him, they will kill Him; and the third day He will rise again." Luke 18:31-33

Even then, Luke writes that they missed it. Yahweh had come to be *with them.* That Jesus had something totally *other* in mind was not something a physical feel and touch world could accept or conceptualize. But the not-so-subtle hints kept coming:

"But now I am going to Him who sent Me; and none of you asks Me, 'Where are You going?' But because I have said these things to you, sorrow has filled your heart. But I tell you the truth, it is to your advantage that I go away; for if I do not go away, the Helper will not come to you; but if I go, I will send Him to you." Jn. 16:5-7

Nothing about this to their minds was jiving with a long-awaited Messiah that had come to not only deliver them, but to bless them, and to BE WITH THEM. You can't be *with us* if You're leaving us, so obviously He must be referring to something else—right???

A HIGH VALUE

It speaks to one of our highest—often unspoken—values. *Companionship.* Admittedly, I tend to be an introvert. Not a hermit kind of introvert, but an *I need some quiet alone time to recharge* kind of introvert. And yet, if you can believe it, none of the books I've written or the events I've planned have been done from a quiet secluded place. People with vivid imaginations don't do well with too blank a canvas. So, nearly everything significant I do is done in crowded places---Starbucks, Panera, Barnes & Noble, etc. I function well **alone** in a crowd. It has made me a bit of a conundrum to friends and acquaintances, but I've learned to accept it.

Meanwhile, introvert or no, I need companionship. EVERYONE DOES. Even the hermit. We're simply designed that way. Without it, we become emotionally unhealthy and quite frankly, useless. To that end, I cannot express my gratitude for Stephanie and my children. In a word or three—I NEED THEM! To those spouses who have busied themselves to the point of becoming strangers in their own homes and now wonder why intimacy is hard to come by, I can only say to you that I married Stephanie Coleson Reid to be *WITH HER.* Maybe let that thought marinate for a bit.

In companionship, ***with*** is the operative word. *With* brings security, power, and confidence to any relationship. It just does. And now Jesus, who had been *with them* for three and a half years was telling them He was leaving? No—*couldn't be.*

Any naive hopes and delusions of grandeur were crushed when Jesus was arrested and crucified. I understand the difficulty to fully appreciate what this meant to those men and women that had given everything to follow Him. How do you reconcile a man that had healed grotesque deformities, even raising individuals from the dead—making promises of a glorious future—now cold in a grave. Stunned, overwrought disillusionment is not enough.

But then again, how can we appreciate the resurrection three days later in the face of such emotions. Wow! The Jesus that had loved them—taught them—laughed, and even cried with them—was gone—and now BACK AGAIN! (Jn. 20:19-20)

Absolutely, this was it, right? *"Ha—good one, Jesus. We see what you did there. That whole, 'I'm going away business'..... Whew... You had me going there for a bit. Thought You had left us for good. You know... we had everything riding on You... You did know that, right?..."*

Yes, He did. But the Mystery was still hanging in the air. Approximately forty days later, on Mt. Olivet, He would say goodbye again. This time, seemingly forever—but with a strange command and promise. They were to stay together in Jerusalem until they were filled with power (Luke 24:49) and that He would *be with them always.* (Matthew 28:20).

Sorry for pointing this out, and perhaps I have tendency for overthinking things. I can't help but think they were thinking it too.... When You say, *I will be with you always*—just how exactly, are You planning on doing that?—assuming You're speaking literally here, and not merely in a memory sort of way. Because, if it's the memory kind of way, I'm not sure how well that will stand up to crises and bouts of real loneliness when I need *You* and not just a memory.

The answer would come not long after.

THE GIFT — AND A FEW OF MY FAVORITE THINGS

When the day of Pentecost had come, they were all together in one place. And suddenly there came from heaven a noise like a violent rushing wind, and it filled the whole house where they were sitting. And there appeared to them tongues as of fire distributing themselves, and they rested on each one of them. And they were all filled with the Holy Spirit and began to speak with other tongues, as the Spirit was giving them utterance. Acts 2:1-4

Paul called it a *mystery* which was *Christ in you, the hope of glory.* (Col. 1:27) Joel had spoken of it nearly 800 years before. "It will come about after this that I will pour out My Spirit on all mankind; And your sons and daughters will prophesy, your old men will dream dreams, your young men will see visions. Even on the male and female servants I will pour out My Spirit in those days." (Joel 2:28-32)

The voice of Yahweh, through Hosea, had been whispering down through the centuries. The *buy back* was never going to be enough. He wanted to be

WITH US—and He couldn't be more ***with us*** than by being ***IN US!!!***

Andrew Murray wrote in *The Spirit of Christ:*

> The distinction is of the deepest importance. In the new Spirit given to me, I have a work of God in me; in God's Spirit given, I have God Himself, a Living Person, to dwell with me. What a difference between having a home built by a rich friend, given me to live in, while I remain poor and feeble, or having the rich friend himself come to live with me, and fulfill my every want![25]

It really was—*is*—the gift that keeps on giving. Jesus—*in me*—every day of the year. A few of my *favorite things...:* Counselor for all seasons. A Teacher for every moment. A celebrating and weeping friend for the happenings of my days. Not with divided attention—but *all there, all the time.* The Jesus that was laid in the manger, nailed to the cross, risen from the dead, ascended to heaven, now living in ME!

MERRY CHRISTMAS!!!!!!!!

---

[25] Andrew Murray. *The Spirit of Christ,* (Fort Washington, PA: Christian Literature, 1963), 18.

CHAPTER TWELVE

UNFORNICATE your world UNDER the COMMAND of your KING

Dear friends—those who have recognized Jesus for who He claimed to be, and have surrendered your life to Him and are now living with Jesus *living inside of you*: How will we hold the Christmas celebration? Like children, anxiously looking for the next gift, eager to see how we'll make out in it all, maybe mesmerized by the bright lights that flicker around us, lost in our own heads? Or perhaps we will come to feel it the way Yahweh has felt it. Can we be vulnerable enough to let that thought in—with the emotions and reality checks that are soon to follow—with blinding light that illuminates a world in need?

Will we remember that:

"Long lay the world in sin and error pining

Till He appeared and the **soul felt its worth?"**[26] (bold and italics mine)

OUR WORLD AT CHRISTMAS TIME

In 2016, 827,261 marriages in the United States ended in divorce.[27] To put that in perspective, 1,654,522 people had their hearts broken, abused, neglected, hurt. The numbers for 2018 aren't looking any better. By all accounts, divorce is hell for those who endure it. The misery grows exponentially when the collateral damage done to children, family, and friends are factored in.

Did you know that 95,730 rapes were reported in the U.S. for 2016 as well?[28] It is commonly believed that this number would sky rocket if unreported numbers were added to it. Nearly 100,000 women suffering trauma of the worst kind. Social anxiety abounding—trust and confidence often shattered. We often fail to also consider the issues of the assailants. What traumas, abuse, neglect, lack of discipline, led them to the place where they could do such things?

---

[26] *Oh Holy Night.* **1847** - 1847 w. Placide Clappeau, French, English translation John S. Dwight, m. Adolphe C. Adam.

[27] https://www.divorcemag.com/articles/us-divorce-statistics-and-divorce-rate-2016-2017/

[28] https://www.fbi.gov/news/stories/2016-crime-statistics-released

Also in 2016, an estimated 7.9 million property crimes were reported, resulting in some $15.6 billion dollars in losses.[29] Why does it happen? Need and want perverted. People and families are rendered paranoid while perpetrators of the crimes hold what they have in fear or search for justifications for the damage they've done.

In what has to feel like the ultimate in tragedies, 17,284 homicides were reported in 2017.[30] Nothing is more final, more complete, than to have someone you love taken. Not by causes one might expect, but by the hand of another human being. How do you pick up the pieces? How do you make sense of it? As for those who cross the penultimate line—where does your soul go for comfort and resolution? Maybe it's not a big deal for the sociopath, but most are not. For many, reconciling the deed never comes. The guilty stain remains on the emotion even when the legal sentences are handed out.

Even for the families of the victims—regardless of the offender's sentence—death or life in prison—there's never enough justice to bring their love—their friend back.

Right now, *The Global Slavery Index* reports that as many as 400,000 individuals could be living in slavery

---

[29] https://www.fbi.gov/news/stories/2016-crime-statistics-released

[30]https://www.statista.com/statistics/195331/number-of-murders-in-the-us-by-state/

in the U.S.[31] You read that correctly—the United States of America—home of the *free?* Every year now, for the past eight years we have visited a particular children's home in a major U.S. city that is housing and rehabilitating U.S. born girls that are being rescued from sex trafficking. It's a thing. When you hear their stories and the delusions many of them live under, your heart can't help but fall into indignant rage.

Staying close to home ——

72,000 drug overdoses were reported in 2017.[32] Who knows how many went unreported. In 2009, my wife had the displeasure of wheeling untold numbers of individuals from the ER to the psychiatric ward, where she worked as a nurse assistant/tech. The despair on the faces of the family members who brought them told you all you needed to know. More than a few were repeat visitors. The question oft repeated—*"where was rock bottom?"* Sadly, many find it to be final. Too final for their families and loved ones to bear.

Increasing numbers of the U.S. population no longer know how to cope with life-living without the help of a drug. A recent report revealed antidepressant use had jumped sixty-five percent in fifteen years. They estimate as much as thirteen percent of the current

---

[31] https://www.theguardian.com/world/2018/jul/19/us-modern-slavery-report-global-slavery-index

[32] https://www.drugabuse.gov/related-topics/trends-statistics/overdose-death-rates

population is using some form of antidepressant.[33] Am I mentioning this to shame those in need of medical solutions? Absolutely not! I bring it to your attention to illustrate the disillusionment with living that is escalating rampantly in our culture.

In connection to that, an estimated 2.8% of U.S. adults have been diagnosed with bipolar disorder in the past year (2017).[34] I don't care how *half-full* your glass is, that's a large number of real people with real seemingly inconsolable emotional and mental pain.

Is it any wonder then that 44,965 suicides were recorded in 2016?[35] Unfortunately, no numbers are available to provide a definitive number for suicide attempts. However, in 2015, we do know that 505,507 people visited a hospital for injuries due to self-harm.[36] That's nearly enough to fill the *Big House*—Michigan University's football stadium—five times!

We haven't even gotten to those undiagnosed but depressed or experiencing anxiety in their jobs, to those facing foreclosures, dealing with lives lived differently than they had dreamed for themselves. We haven't touched on the poor suffering the indignities of

---

[33] https://medicalxpress.com/news/2017-08-antidepressant-percent-years.html

[34] https://www.nimh.nih.gov/health/statistics/bipolar-disorder.shtml

[35] https://afsp.org/suicide-rate-1-8-percent-according-recent-cdc-data-year-2016/

[36] https://afsp.org/about-suicide/suicide-statistics/

the welfare state, the overextended, in over their heads upper middle class, drowning in debt, while keeping up with the Jones's. The boyfriend—girlfriend break-ups. The cheated on. The cheaters. The angry. The careless and reckless, leaving collateral damage everywhere they go. Or the anxious young girl hiding her social fears as best she can, the teen living in constant turmoil from bullies. Those employing defense mechanisms of every kind to survive the relationships and circumstances of their everyday living.

Is that enough???

A very well-known national speaker once quipped at a conference for a somewhat prominent evangelical group of pastors. "*The kids in our inner cities are fucked up—and the sad thing is, many of you are more upset that I just said 'fucked up' than the fact that they actually are!*"

He wasn't invited back—*but He wasn't wrong.*

Are you aware that you carry a message of worth that the soul can feel?

You do.

WHY THE SALVATION ARMY BELL STILL RINGS AT CHRISTMAS

The statistics and real-life tragedies above represent souls—emotion, intellect, and will—fornicated to the places they desperately seek for answers. They illustrate *need* and *want* run amuck, slaying at will. Some of the deaths are slow, hardly to be noticed, but death all the same. Others are painful in the living and watching—*and you carry the remedy for all of it.* The gift you received, the gift you carry, is for ALL OF THEM.

Do you understand it's why the Salvation Army bell still rings after all these years? Need is universal. The damage—personal and collateral—is universal as well. The call—the remedy—the gift—the *buy back* has been given.

Will you share it?

Will you also freely give it away?

UNFORNICATE your world UNDER the COMMAND of your KING

It's what Jesus wanted. It's the last word He would physically speak with His human mouth on planet earth. "Go therefore and make disciples of all the nations, baptizing them in the name of the Father and the Son and the Holy Spirit, teaching them to observe all that I commanded you; and lo, I am with you always, even to the end of the age." (Matthew 28:19-20)

*Go and **unfornicate** your friends—your loved ones—your neighbors—your co-workers—those in foreign lands—neighborhoods you typically don't hangout in—the bars you visit—the community events you* *attend: EVERYWHERE YOU GO* ***under*** *the* ***command*** *of your* ***King.***

For truly He taught us to love one another
His law is love and His gospel is peace
Chains He shall break
For the slave is our brother
And in His Name
All oppression shall cease

Sweet hymns of joy
In grateful chorus raise we
Let all within us praise His holy Name

Christ is the Lord
O praise His Name forever
His power and glory
Evermore proclaim
His power and glory
Evermore proclaim[37] (bold print mine)

MERRY CHRISTMAS!!!

Oh, and uhh...welcome to the secret handshake, friend.

Go and ***unfuck your world!***

---

[37] *Oh Holy Night.* **1847** - 1847 w. Placide Clappeau, French, English translation John S. Dwight, m. Adolphe C. Adam.

an invitation

Scott and I discussed this last section at length and decided to write it together. I am his wife, Stephanie, and so glad you read through. I'm with Scott for a few gifted days in a mountain condo near Boone, NC to help complete and edit this Christmas story. I've been killing him with that way too early holiday music (it's late October though, come on..) No joke, though, every time I came to a song reference, I searched it and hit play..the Whos' "Welcome Christmas" is playing right now because..it's just the best.

As I mentioned in the Foreword, I read this out loud to him on this mountain. I think he was into it too, because he was laugh-crying in some of the parts that I couldn't quite get through without tissue. He's held the story close for quite some time, and to TELL IT is a gift.

The thing is—all this outlining and researching and telling is pointless unless it CHANGES YOU—and forever the way you see Christmas (like it has changed him—and me).

It strikes us that it may be obviously written to readers who already know a lot about the Bible or who have grown up in North American "church world." We both do—and did—so it's what we know and how we write. And to you —> the reader who also **does** and **did**: our prayer (and this invitation) is that chapters one through eleven remix the STORY and LIGHT YOU UP again (and maybe light an ember of interest in the ambiguous and complex OT prophetic books)—and that chapter twelve wrecks you to the core for the world you LIVE. That you will go use alllll of the crazy gifts God has given you and strength He has placed in you to spend your days unFornicating under the Consent—or Command, he said in the end—of your King. Prayers and more prayers to that end, dear friend.

To those of you who have read through who did **not** already know any of this and/or who did **not** grow up in any sort of church world:

This is an invitation to respond to the God of Hosea who wants to buy you back and unFornicate your world. He wants to be in relationship with you. His Word says He is love (1 John 4). That He loves the world. (John 3:16) That He demonstrates His love for us, in that while we were yet sinners, Christ died for us. (Rom. 5:8) That we're like the lost sheep. (He'll leave the 99 to go after us if we wander off. Look it up! Matthew 18:12)

Jesus said to the crowds on the dusty roads and hills of Palestine that He was the WAY, the TRUTH, and the LIFE. He told them that He was the way to the Father. (John 14:6) He told them to come to Him for rest. (Matthew 11:28-30) He told a religious leader who came to Him in secret at night that he needed to be born again (a kind of mystery—but a spiritual birth/newness and leaving behind his other life). (John 3). He has spoken through inspired biblical writers that all have sinned and fallen short (Rom. 3:23), and that sin earns death but that His free gift is eternal life through Christ! (Rom. 6:23) That confessing that He is Lord and heart-believing that God raised Him from the dead brings salvation (Rom. 10:9-10). Salvation from death—which is really the disconnect and aloneness and separation from the One who was willing to buy you back that has made you feel empty up until now.

Friend, if you have felt FUBAR (I didn't look it up, but he told me what I missed because I only rode the school bus one year in junior high and mine was the first stop. Never have I ever heard that until I read it in chapter seven.) If you have felt F***ed Up Beyond All Recognition: HE IS REMEDY. He lived a sinless life, was crucified for you, and came back to life (don't think Frosty this time—think real life HE WAS WRAPPED IN GRAVE CLOTHES FOR THREE DAYS IN A TOMB and then He walked away and 500+ people saw Him alive!!), and—He PURSUES you. John 15:16 says, "You did not choose Me but I chose you.."

If you hadn't really spent much time thinking about Jesus or that there was any real reason for you to think about Him—and this book has got you thinking about Him—here are the rest of Scott's thoughts/invitation—(and how to RSVP):

Yahweh (the Hebrew name for the God of the Bible) is unlike any other deity worshiped on the planet. In reality, Yahweh pursues you, because He loves you—desires relationship with you. In every other religion, man is left to guess, grope, and search for the favor of his god.

So much concerning this relationship hinges on *agreement—acknowledgement.*

Paul writes in Romans 3:23, "for all have sinned and fall short of the glory of God." If you paid attention to our definition of sin earlier in the book, this shouldn't be offensive to you. I'll paraphrase, just in case you forgot: *For all hurt themselves or somebody else emotionally, physically, mentally, or spiritually.* They say the first step to recovery is to admit you have a problem. This is one of those moments where we simply agree.

Again, Paul writes, “For the wages of sin is death, but the free gift of God is eternal life in Christ Jesus our Lord.” (Romans 6:23) The laws—rules if you will, recorded in the Old Testament were never arbitrary measuring devices to ascertain worthiness. God is a creator. Creation operates by design—secularists even refer to some of them as laws of nature. The laws were the optimal operating manuals for living. By consequence, similar to ignoring car maintenance tips, if you violate them, you or someone else, will in point of fact, get hurt.

Hurt brings death. But the death it is speaking of here is not necessarily the death you’re thinking of. Death is, in reality, separation from God. While sin does ultimately lead to the hurt and death of your birthday suit—the greater tragedy is the separation from God that you were born into—for which Jesus has paid to redeem you.

“The Lord is near to all who call upon Him, to all who call upon Him in truth.” (Psalm 145:18)

“The word is near you, in your mouth and in your heart”—that is, the word of faith which we are preaching, that if you confess with your mouth Jesus as Lord, and believe in your heart that God raised Him from the dead, you will be saved; for with the heart a person believes, resulting in righteousness, and with the mouth he confesses, resulting in salvation. Romans 10:8-10

It brings us back to agreeing. That's ultimately what confessing means. We confess—*agree* that Jesus is everything He claims to be. Never God little g, but God big G. Hope you notice the sincerity involved above. Yahweh is after our hearts. We can say we intellectually agree, but hold our hearts in reserve. Friend, if you paid attention to Hosea's story, you will know by now that His love means to have and to bless all of you. If you come to Him like that—you will have Him *because He will have you.*

Belief is such a powerful thing. Yahweh loves it. So should we. The apostle John—one who knew Jesus intimately, wrote, "But as many as received Him, to them He gave the right to become children of God, even to those who believe in His name..." (John 1:12)

If this all makes sense, and if in these moments, you know He is speaking to you, we invite you to have a conversation with Him.

RSVP

Without well thought out words, but just the raw emotion and thoughts that can be spoken safely to a good Father, express your acknowledgement—agreement—and commitment to surrender yourself to Him in your own words. Perhaps to say it more plainly, you can tell Him in your own authentic ways that you agree and have sorrow that you have sinned. That you really do believe Jesus is exactly who He says He is. That you are completely surrendering your life to Him. And that nothing would be better than for His Spirit—the Spirit of Jesus, to come live in you.

If you are ready to do that now and will do that now—there will be no delay in your becoming a son or daughter of the Living God in this moment. For you, the *buy back*—and perpetual *togethernesss* with Jesus will be real and complete—which should make for the Merriest of Christmases you have ever known!

FINAL THOUGHTS WITH OUR LOVE

Well... if you did that... in the words of Frosty the Snowman——**Happy Birthday!!****[38]—and Merry Christmas indeed.**

As for what should be next. I would like to encourage you to find a Bible—maybe not just any Bible. If you're unsure, perhaps you could contact a local Christian bookstore or a trusted Christian friend whom you know is a student of the Bible to ask for their help in getting what you need. Everything you will need to learn about who you have now become and what is available to you will be found in this Book. It's vitally important.

I would like to recommend www.thebibleproject.com—even advise you to frequent the site often as you learn. There are some things about the Bible and throughout the Bible that are initially hard to understand, and it is helpful to have explanation. The Bible Project illustrates the flow of each book really well and is a good guide for simple interpretation as you begin reading. If you're wondering if I have any connection to the folks there—rest assured that at present, I do not. (I'm just a grateful fan.)

---

[38] *Frosty The Snowman.* Directed by Arthur Rankin, Jr. and Jules Bass, Rankin/Bass Productions, 1969.

We also encourage you to find a community of Christians to spend time with. Remember, we were made for community. We pray you may connect with a church that teaches the Bible as the Words of Yahweh without any error.

Above all, spend time with the One who so very much wants to spend time with you. A good family of believers—church—will show you how.

With much love and belief,

Scott Reid

Bibliography

afsp.com. 2018.
https://afsp.org/about-suicide/suicide-statistics/

afsp.com. 2018.
https://afsp.org/suicide-rate-1-8-percent-according-recent-cdc-data-year-2016/

Chisholm, Robert B. Jr. *Interpreting The Minor Prophets.* Grand Rapids, MI: Academie Books, 1990.

divorcemag.com. 2018.
https://www.divorcemag.com/articles/us-divorce-statistics-and-divorce-rate-2016-2017/

drugabuse.com. 2018.
https://www.drugabuse.gov/related-topics/trends-statistics/overdose-death-rates

fbi.gov. 2018.
https://www.fbi.gov/news/stories/2016-crime-statistics-released

Lasor, William Sanford, David Allen Hubbard, and Frederic W. M. Bush. *Old Testament Survey.* Grand Rapids, MI: William B. Eerdmans Publishing, 1996.

Lewis, C.S. *Chronicles of Narnia.* New York, NY: Harper Collins, 2001.

Lewis, C.S. *Mere Christianity.* SanFrancisco, CA: Harper, 1952.

medicalxpress.com. 2018. https://medicalxpress.com/news/2017-08-antidepressant-percent-years.html

Murray, Andrew. *The Spirit of Christ.* Fort Washington, PA: Christian Literature Crusade, 1963.

nimph.nih.gov. 2018. https://www.nimh.nih.gov/health/statistics/bipolar-disorder.shtml

Otis, George Jr. *The Twilight Labyrinth.* Grand Rapids, MI: Chosen Books, 1997.

Pascal, Blaise. *Pascal's Pensees,* trans. W.F. Trotter, New York: E.P. Dutton, 1958.

Reed, Oscar F., Armor D. Peisker, H. Ray Dunning, and William M. Greathouse. *Beacon Bible Commentary, Vol. 5, Hosea Through Malachi.* Kansas City, MI: Beacon Hill Press. 1966.

Reid, Tsion Scott. "Not So Silent Night." Unpublished. 2017.

statista.com. 2018. https://www.statista.com/statistics/195331/number-of-murders-in-the-us-by-state/

Strong, James. *The Strongest NASB Exhaustive Concordance.* Grand Rapids, MI: Zondervan, 2000.

theguardian.com. 2018.
https://www.theguardian.com/world/2018/jul/19/us-modern-slavery-report-global-slavery-index

---

Discography

A Merry Christmas. Arthur Warrell. 1935, Oxford University Press.

David Crowder Band. *Oh For Joy*. Sparrow Records – 5099994636529, sixstepsrecords – 5099994636529, 2011, compact disc.

Frosty The Snowman. Directed by Arthur Rankin, Jr. and Jules Bass, Rankin/Bass Productions, 1969.

God Rest Ye Merry Gentleman. **ca. 1760** - w.m. English Traditional.

How The Grinch Stole Christmas. Directed by Chuck Jones. MGM Animation/Visual Arts. 1966.

It's A Wonderful Life. Frank Capra, RKO Radio Pictures, 1946.

McMillan, John Mark. *The Medicine*. Integrity Music – 48152. 2010. *Compact Disc.*
Copyright © 2005 Integrity's Hosanna! Music (ASCAP) (adm. at CapitolCMGPublishing.com) All rights reserved. Used by permission.

Oh Come Emmanuel. **1850s** - w. translation John Mason Neale, Henry Sloane Coffin, m. French Hymn, 1400s

Oh Holy Night. **1847** - 1847 w. Placide Clappeau, French, English translation John S. Dwight, m. Adolphe C. Adam.

What Child Is This. **1865** - 1865 - William C. Dix, m. 16th Century English Traditional

What's Opera Doc?. Chuck Jones. Warner Bros. Cartoons. 1957.

Current and future projects from Scott and Stephanie Reid for 121 Resources:

Going In Circles And Actually Getting Somewhere

Available now

Still Going in Circles And Getting Somewhere

Sequel to the above
Available soon

Jack and Jill Series

Case study series that will address specific topics and life circumstances using the tools given in *Still Going in Circles and Getting Somewhere.*
In queue after the sequel above!

You can support 121 resources // mission projects and book Scott to speak at www.ph121.org.

121 Inc., P.O. Box 26, Wallburg, NC 27373

CPSIA information can be obtained
at www.ICGtesting.com
Printed in the USA
BVHW042210201218
536143BV00020B/634/P

9 781730 786365